U.S. ENVIRONMENTAL PROTECTION AGENCY

OFFICE OF INSPECTOR GENERAL

Examination of Costs Claimed Under EPA Cooperative Agreement 2A-83440701 Awarded Under the Recovery Act to Cascade Sierra Solutions, Eugene, Oregon

Report No. 12-R-0749   **September 4, 2012**

Scan this code to
learn more about
the EPA OIG.

Report Contributors: Michael Owen
                                             Darren Schorer
                                             John Burns
                                             Eileen Collins

Abbreviations

CA	Cooperative Agreement
CARB	California Air Resources Board
CFR	Code of Federal Regulations
CSS	Cascade Sierra Solutions
DERA	Diesel Emissions Reduction Act
EPA	U.S. Environmental Protection Agency
FY	Fiscal year
FTE	Full-time equivalent
MY	Model year
OIG	Office of Inspector General
OMB	Office of Management and Budget
Recovery Act	American Recovery and Reinvestment Act of 2009

Cover photo: Example of an EPA certified SmartWay tractor. (EPA photo)

U.S. Environmental Protection Agency
Office of Inspector General

12-R-0749
September 4, 2012

At a Glance

Why We Did This Review

The U.S. Environmental Protection Agency (EPA), Office of Inspector General, reviewed the amounts drawn by Cascade Sierra Solutions (CSS) under Cooperative Agreement (CA) 2A-83440701. The purpose of the audit was to determine whether CSS complied with federal requirements and terms and conditions for Diesel Emission Reduction Act grants or cooperative agreements awarded under the American Recovery and Reinvestment Act of 2009 (Recovery Act). EPA awarded the CA to CSS in August 2009 under the Recovery Act. The CA provides $9 million to create a revolving loan program for heavy duty diesel trucks to save fuel and reduce emissions.

This report addresses the following EPA Goal or Cross-Cutting Strategy:

* *Taking action on climate change and improving air quality*

For further information, contact our Office of Congressional and Public Affairs at (202) 566-2391.

The full report is at:
www.epa.gov/oig/reports/2012/
20120904-12-R-0749.pdf

Examination of Costs Claimed Under EPA Cooperative Agreement 2A-83440701 Awarded Under the Recovery Act to Cascade Sierra Solutions, Eugene, Oregon

What We Found

CSS' financial management system did not support that funds drawn are reasonable, allocable, and allowable in accordance with applicable laws, regulations, and CA terms and conditions. In particular, CSS':

* Financial management system pertaining to cash draws, revolving fund accounting, project costs, and progress reporting does not meet the requirements of the Code of Federal Regulations (CFR) under 40 CFR Part 30 and 2 CFR Part 230, and the CA.
* Procurements did not meet competition or cost and price analysis requirements of 40 CFR Part 30, the recipient's procurement policy, or CA requirements.
* Reporting of the number of jobs created or retained with Recovery Act funds did not comply with Office of Management and Budget guidance.

As a result, we are unable to provide an opinion on the financial resources, related liabilities, revenue, expenses, and residual balances of the CA-funded revolving loan program. Therefore, we have questioned the $9 million drawn under the CA as unallowable costs.

Recommendations and Planned Agency Corrective Actions

We recommend that the Director for the Office of Grants and Debarment disallow and recover $9 million in questioned costs; consider suspension and debarment of CSS on current and future awards; require CSS to ensure that the use of funds meets federal criteria; require special conditions for future awards to CSS; and provide clarifying guidance to CSS on progress reporting requirements. We also recommend that the Director require CSS to comply with pertinent procurement requirements; disallow pre-2007 model year trucks as project costs; and assist CSS with developing a methodology to calculate number of jobs created and direct CSS to correct the numbers reported, with documentation. The Agency generally agreed with the findings and said that it has initiated corrective actions to address some of the weaknesses identified in the report. CSS disagreed with most of the findings and two of the recommendations. CSS partially agreed with one recommendation and neither agreed nor disagreed with six recommendations. CSS described actions planned to document compliance with EPA procurement regulations and is willing to work with EPA on developing a Recovery Act job reporting methodology.

UNITED STATES ENVIRONMENTAL PROTECTION AGENCY
WASHINGTON, D.C. 20460

September 4, 2012

MEMORANDUM

SUBJECT: Examination of Costs Claimed Under EPA Cooperative Agreement 2A-83440701 Awarded Under the Recovery Act to Cascade Sierra Solutions, Eugene, Oregon Report No. 12-R-0749

FROM: Arthur A. Elkins, Jr.

TO: Howard Corcoran
Director, Office of Grants and Debarment
Office of Administration and Resources Management

This is our report on the subject examination conducted by the Office of Inspector General (OIG) of the U.S. Environmental Protection Agency (EPA). This report contains findings that describe the problems the OIG has identified and corrective actions the OIG recommends. This report represents the opinion of the OIG and does not necessarily represent the final EPA position. EPA managers in accordance with established audit resolution procedures will make final determinations on matters in this report.

We performed this examination as part of our responsibility under the American Recovery and Reinvestment Act of 2009 (Recovery Act). The purpose of our examination was to determine whether the amounts drawn by Cascade Sierra Solutions (CSS) under Cooperative Agreement 2A-83440701 were reasonable, allocable, and allowable in accordance with federal requirements and terms and conditions for Diesel Emission Reduction Act grants awarded under the Recovery Act. CSS received $9 million in Recovery Act funds under the EPA award.

Action Required

In accordance with EPA Manual 2750, Chapter 3, Section 6(f), you are required to provide us your proposed management decision for resolution of the findings contained in this report before you formally complete resolution with the recipient. As part of the audit resolution process, your proposed decision is due in 120 days, or on January 2, 2013. To expedite the resolution process, please e-mail an electronic version of your proposed management decision to adachi.robert@epa.gov.

Your response will be posted on the OIG's public website, along with our memorandum commenting on your response. Your response should be provided as an Adobe PDF file that complies with the accessibility requirements of Section 508 of the Rehabilitation Act of 1973, as amended. The final response should not contain data that you do not want to be released to the public; if your response contains such data, you should identify the data for redaction or removal. We have no objection to the further release of this report to the public. This report will be available at http://www.epa.gov/oig.

If you or your staff have any questions regarding this report, please contact Melissa Heist, Assistant Inspector General for Audit, at (202) 566-0899 or heist.melissa@epa.gov; or Robert Adachi, Product Line Director, at (415) 947-4537 or adachi.robert@epa.gov.

Examination of Costs Claimed Under
EPA Cooperative Agreement 2A-83440701 Awarded Under the
Recovery Act to Cascade Sierra Solutions, Eugene, Oregon

12-R-0749

Table of Contents

Chapters

Appendices

Chapter 1
Independent Attestation Report

As part of our oversight of cooperative agreement (CA) awards by the U.S. Environmental Protection Agency (EPA), we have examined Cascade Sierra Solutions' (CSS') compliance with the requirements of the Code of Federal Regulations (CFR) under 2 CFR Part 230, *Cost Principles for Non-Profit Organizations*; 40 CFR Part 30, *Uniform Administrative Requirements for Grants and Agreements with Institutions of Higher Education, Hospitals, and Other Non-Profit Organizations*; and the American Recovery and Reinvestment Act of 2009 (Recovery Act) applicable to the outlays for CA 2A-83440701. By accepting the funding provided through the CA, CSS has responsibility for complying with these requirements. Our responsibility is to express an opinion on CSS' compliance based on our examination.

Our examination was conducted in accordance with generally accepted government auditing standards issued by the Comptroller General of the United States and the attestation standards established by the American Institute of Certified Public Accountants. We examined, on a test basis, evidence supporting management's assertion and performed such other procedures as we considered necessary in the circumstances. We believe that our examination provides a reasonable basis for our opinion.

We contacted EPA's Office of Transportation and Air Quality as well as the Grants and Interagency Agreements Management Division in EPA's Office of Grants and Debarment within the Office of Administration and Resources Management, and the Office of General Counsel. We gathered information on criteria relevant to the CA; obtained an understanding of the proposed revolving loan fund; and gathered information concerning CSS' performance. Specifically, we performed the following steps:

- Reviewed the request for application associated with award of CA 2A-83440701.
- Reviewed CA 2A-83440701 awarded to CSS and its modifications.
- Reviewed CSS' work plan.
- Reviewed 2 CFR Part 230 and 40 CFR Part 30.
- Conducted interviews with EPA's project officer for the CA.

We made site visits to CSS' office in Eugene, Oregon, and performed the following steps:

- Reviewed requests for reimbursement to EPA under the CA to determine whether the draws complied with federal requirements and were disbursed for expenditures allocable to the CA.
- Reviewed CSS' progress report for the quarter ending December 31, 2010, to obtain an understanding of the financial status and activities of the revolving loan program.
- Selected a judgmental sample of $4,336,066 in expenditures that CSS associated with the $9 million in cash drawn under the CA. We reviewed supporting invoices, payment documents, and associated accounting system entries to determine whether the expenditures were allocable and allowable under 40 CFR Part 30 and the CA.
- Selected a judgmental sample of 4 of 798 projects listed in CSS' progress report for the quarter ending December 31, 2010, to determine whether costs were allowable under 2 CFR Part 230, 40 CFR Part 30, and the CA. The sample represented $229,350 of $47,918,615 in total project costs reported to EPA. We did not expand the sample because of material deficiencies with CSS' financial management system.
- Reviewed CSS' chart of accounts and general ledger detail to determine whether the revolving fund program activity was segregated within the accounting system.
- Selected a judgmental sample of 4 of 27 completed truck procurement actions exceeding $100,000 that CSS identified as allocable to the CA-funded revolving loan program. The sample represented $3,303,337 of the $10,477,704 in total costs for the 27 procurement actions. We reviewed all available supporting documentation for the sample of truck procurements to determine whether CSS met applicable requirements of 40 CFR Part 30.
- Selected a judgmental sample of 11 of 472 emission control equipment procurements. The sample represented $163,193 of $4,987,923 in total costs reported by CSS for the 472 procurements. We reviewed all available supporting documentation for the sample to determine whether CSS met applicable requirements of 40 CFR Part 30. We did not expand the sample because of material deficiencies with CSS' financial management system.
- Conducted interviews of CSS' personnel to gain an understanding of the organization's accounting system, internal controls, and costs reported under the CA.

We reviewed other prior independent reviews of CSS' financial management system for the CA. We reviewed CSS' 2009 audit required under the Single Audit Act Amendments of 1996 and draft financial statements for 2010. As part of the review, we interviewed the public accounting firm performing the single audit to gain a complete understanding of the scope of the 2009 single audit. We reviewed a 2010 report on a limited scope financial management system review of CSS performed for EPA's Office of Transportation and Air Quality. We also reviewed the supporting working papers to obtain a complete understanding of the scope and results of the evaluation.

We conducted our audit work between March 2011 and December 2011. Our examination disclosed material noncompliance and internal control weaknesses with financial management. In particular, CSS':

- Financial management system pertaining to cash draws, revolving fund accounting, project costs, and progress reporting does not meet the requirements of 40 CFR Part 30, 2 CFR Part 230, and the CA.
- Procurements did not meet competition or cost and price analysis requirements of 40 CFR Part 30, the recipient's procurement policy, or CA requirements.
- Reporting of the number of jobs created or retained with Recovery Act funds did not comply with Office of Management and Budget (OMB) reporting guidance.

As a result, we are unable to provide an opinion on the financial resources, related liabilities, revenue, expenses, and residual balances of the CA-funded revolving loan program. Therefore, we have questioned the $9 million drawn under the CA as unallowable costs and recommend that EPA recover these funds from CSS.

In our opinion, because of the effect of the issues described above, CSS has not complied with federal requirements for the grant period ending December 31, 2010.

Robert K. Adachi
Director for Forensic Audits
September 4, 2012

Chapter 2
Introduction

Purpose

EPA's Office of Inspector General (OIG) conducted this review to determine whether the amounts drawn by CSS under CA 2A-83440701 were reasonable, allocable, and allowable in accordance with federal requirements and terms and conditions for Diesel Emission Reduction Act (DERA) grants awarded under the Recovery Act.

Background

DERA was signed into law in August 2005 under Title VII, Subtitle G, of the Energy Policy Act of 2005. DERA authorized $200 million per year from fiscal years (FYs) 2007 to 2011 (or a total of $1 billion) for EPA to fund programs to achieve significant reductions in diesel emission in terms of tons of pollution produced and diesel emission exposures, particularly from fleets operating in areas designated by the Agency as poor air quality areas. Of the authorized DERA amount, 70 percent is authorized for competitive national grant and low cost revolving loans, as determined by the EPA Administrator. The remaining 30 percent is for state grant and loan programs. Congress appropriated a total of $169.2 million for EPA under DERA for FYs 2008 through 2010. Congress appropriated an additional $300 million to EPA in FY 2009 for DERA grants under the Recovery Act.

EPA awarded CA 2A-83440701 on August 24, 2009, to CSS through the DERA SmartWay Clean Diesel Finance Program. EPA's SmartWay Clean Diesel Finance Program issues grants to establish innovative financing programs for buyers of eligible diesel or alternatively fueled vehicles and equipment. The purpose of the award to CSS was to provide federal assistance of $9 million in Recovery Act funds to create a national revolving loan program for heavy-duty trucks (trucks) to save fuel and reduce emissions. The grant budget and project period was from August 1, 2009, to October 31, 2011. As of December 31, 2010, CSS had drawn down all $9 million.

CSS, based in Eugene, Oregon, is a non-profit organization with a mission to save fuel and reduce emissions from heavy duty diesel engines. CSS promotes EPA SmartWay-verified technologies and products certified by the California Air Resources Board, as well as emerging technologies, that have been shown to provide quantifiable emission reduction benefits. CSS assists truck owners to finance clean diesel solutions using state, federal, and private sources of funding. Table 1 identifies some of the sources of CSS' funding as of December 31, 2010.

Table 1: Partial list of CSS funding sources

Source	Award amount
EPA Region 1	$1,148,236
EPA Region 2	1,404,327
EPA Region 6	1,150,228
EPA Region 8	850,000
EPA Region 10	907,072
EPA SmartWay 1	1,130,000
EPA SmartWay 2 (CA 2A-83440701)	9,000,000
EPA SmartWay 3	2,000,000
Puget Sound Clean Air Authority	2,000,000
City of Sacramento Congestion Mitigation and Air Quality	200,000
California Proposition 1B	19,335,000
U.S. Department of Energy	22,200,000
Total	$61,324,863

Source: Schedule of federal, state, and local awards as of December 31, 2010, provided by CSS.

CSS provides operators with truck replacements and SmartWay equipment upgrades that are intended to reduce fuel consumption and emissions through the CA-funded revolving loan program. CSS' revolving loan program focuses on providing truck replacements and equipment upgrades to operators through lease-to-own agreements. CSS intends to replenish the revolving loan fund through payments made under the lease-to-own agreements.

Chapter 3
Financial Management System Does Not Meet Federal Requirements

CSS' financial management system does not meet federal requirements that apply under the EPA CA award. Specifically:

- Cash draws did not comply with 40 CFR Part 30.22, Appendix A of 2 CFR Part 230, or the terms and conditions of the CA.
- A formal revolving fund has not been established to support the revolving loan program specified by the CA or to meet the requirements of 40 CFR Part 30.21.
- Revolving loan program projects costs and associated lessee payments were not fully supported as required by 40 CFR Part 30.21 and Appendix A of 2 CFR Part 230.
- The progress report for the quarter ending December 2010 did not accurately identify expenditures by funding source, the number of projects, and the total cost of projects in the revolving fund program.

As a result, CSS is unable to support that all funds drawn under the CA were used for expenditures that are allowable under and allocable to the CA. We are also unable to provide an opinion on the financial resources, related liabilities, revenue, expenses, and residual balances of the revolving fund. Therefore, we question the $9 million drawn under the CA as unallowable costs and recommend that EPA recover these funds from CSS. EPA should also consider suspension and debarment proceedings against CSS. We found that the financial management issues were primarily caused by CSS' underestimating accounting system requirements for the revolving fund.

Cash Draws Did Not Meet Federal Requirements

CSS' advance cash draws did not comply with the requirements of 40 CFR Part 30.22, Appendix A of 2 CFR Part 230, or the terms and conditions of the CA. CSS cash draws exceeded immediate cash needs during October and November 2009. In addition, CSS' accounting system information and documentation did not show that the draws were supported by expenditures incurred under the CA. As a result, CSS was required to repay EPA $1,751 in interest income earned on the cash draws and was not able to show that the $9 million in draws were used for expenditures allocable to and allowable under the CA.

Cash Draws Exceeded Cash Needs

CSS drew down the $9 million award over the period from September 2009 through October 2010. For the months of October and November 2009, six of CSS' cash draws exceeded immediate cash needs according to the recipient's records. These cash draws exceeded immediate cash needs by amounts ranging between $510, 257 and $3,141,127, as summarized in table 2 below.

Table 2: Draws in excess of cash needs

Date of draw	Draw amount	Draws in excess of needs (cumulative)
10/01/09	$1,000,000	$510,257
10/07/09	742,000	1,252,257
10/14/09	2,000,000	2,558,257
10/27/09	1,000,000	2,863,497
11/05/09	1,000,000	2,156,127
11/11/09	1,000,000	3,141,127
Total	$6,742,000	

Source: CSS Schedule of Federal Awards

Programmatic Condition 16 of the CA specifies that the recipient may request payment from EPA after it incurs an obligation in accordance with 40 CFR Part 30.22. Under 40 CFR Part 30.22(b), cash advances are limited to the minimum amounts needed and are to be timed in accordance with the actual, immediate cash requirements of the recipient. Title 40 CFR Part 30.22(b) also specifies that the timing and amount of cash advances shall be as close as is administratively feasible to the actual disbursements by the recipient.

According to CSS management, CSS drew cash in advance to have funds available for truck procurements. However, CSS management said that CSS was not able to make some anticipated truck purchases, resulting in the excess CA funds on hand. The issue of excess CA funds on hand was identified during October 2010 as part of a limited scope review conducted for EPA by a contractor. The limited scope review also identified that CSS earned $1,751 of interest on the excess funds. CSS remitted the interest earned on the CA funds to EPA based on the finding of the limited scope review. Under 40 CFR Part 30.22(l), interest earned in excess of $250 must be remitted to the federal government. Therefore, EPA has satisfactorily resolved the interest income issue.

Cash Draws Not Supported as Allocable and Allowable

CSS' accounting system information and documentation did not show that the cash draws were supported by expenditures incurred under the CA. Title 40 CFR Part 30.21(b)(2) specifies that recipient financial management systems shall provide records that identify adequately the source and application of funds for federally sponsored activities. In addition, 2 CFR Part 230, Appendix A, A.2(a) and (g), require costs to be allocable and adequately documented to be considered allowable under an award. Consistent with these regulations, Programmatic Condition 2.5.A of the CA requires the recipient to maintain records that ensure Recovery Act funds are accounted for separately from other grant program funds.

Our review of CSS' accounting system information and bank records showed that the $9 million in draws under the CA were recorded in and deposited to multiple general ledger and bank accounts that included funds from other grant programs. These grant programs were funded through other EPA and various state and local government agreements. For example, CSS initially deposited the $6.7 million of draws listed in table 2 above into a savings account and subsequently transferred 90 percent of these draws between two checking accounts. These three accounts included funding from other sources. These deposit transactions were also recorded in similar savings and checking general ledger accounts that included funding from other sources. Because the CA funding was recorded in and deposited to accounts that included funds from other sources, we were unable to reconcile the $6.7 million in draws with expenditures made under the CA.

We also reviewed a judgmental sample of $4,336,066 in expenditures that CSS associated with the $9 million in cash draws. Our review of invoices, payment documents, and accounting system entries provided by CSS to support the expenditures identified that the documentation and entries did not include notations or coding showing that the costs were incurred under the CA. The documentation and accounting entries only provided information on the type of truck or equipment, cost, and the bank account from which the funds were drawn. Because of these accounting and documentation issues, we were unable to verify that CSS used the $9 million of EPA funding for expenditures that are allocable to and allowable under the CA.

Revolving Loan Fund Requirement Not Met

CSS has not established a formal fund to support the revolving loan program that meets the requirements of 40 CFR Part 30.21. The CA specifies that CSS establish a revolving loan program for heavy-duty trucks to save fuel and reduce emissions with the $9 million award. As discussed earlier in the report, 40 CFR Part 30.21(b)(2) requires recipients' financial management systems to provide records that adequately identify the source and application of funds for federally sponsored activities. Title 40 CFR Part 30.21(b)(3) further specifies that recipients' financial management systems provide accountability for funds, property, and other assets. The CA also provides specific accountability requirements for the award. Programmatic Condition 2.5.A requires the recipient to maintain records that ensure Recovery Act funds are tracked separately from other grant programs. Programmatic Condition 2.7 requires the recipient to maintain effective control over and be accountable for all funds, property, and other assets accrued as a result of the CA.

CSS has not segregated in the accounting system all revenues, costs, cash, and accounts receivables associated with funding provided under the CA from the organization's other programs or operations. CSS had not implemented a project cost system for expenditures made under the CA-funded revolving fund program. CSS did not establish separate accounts for revolving fund transactions during calendar year 2009. CSS recorded revenues, costs, cash, and accounts receivables associated with its revolving fund program to accounts that included transactions from other programs during 2009. During calendar year 2010, CSS used seven dedicated accounts within its accounting system to track revenues and expenses of the revolving fund program separately from other CSS programs and operations. These accounts consisted of one revenue account that contained $78,000 of the $9,000,000 award and six salary and salary-related accounts that totaled $277,431 in expenses. However, the accounts used by CSS in calendar year 2010 did not track all revenues, costs, cash, and accounts receivables associated with the revolving fund program.

Rather than establishing a comprehensive separate set of accounts for the revolving fund program, CSS tracked revolving fund revenues, costs, and lease receivables using spreadsheets. We were not able to reconcile the spreadsheets to the accounting system because most revolving fund transactions were not segregated from other transactions in the system. For example, a spreadsheet provided to us by CSS reporting revolving fund transactions as of December 31, 2010, showed a total lease receivable of $37,037,426. We were unable to verify this total because CSS had not recorded the receivables in a designated revolving fund account(s) in the accounting system. Because CSS has not established and used a comprehensive set of accounts for the revolving fund, we are unable to provide an opinion on the financial resources, related liabilities, revenue, expenses, and residual balances of the fund.

Project Costs Not Fully Supported

CSS was unable to provide complete support for revolving loan program project costs and associated lessee payments as required by Appendix A of 2 CFR Part 230 and 40 CFR Part 30.21. CSS reported in its progress report to EPA for the quarter ending December 31, 2010, that 798 truck and equipment projects with a total cost of $47,918,615 were funded through the revolving loan program. We reviewed a judgmental sample of 4 of the 798 projects to determine if costs were allowable under 2 CFR Part 230, 40 CFR Part 30, and the CA. The sample consisted of CSS truck procurements that were subsequently leased by CSS to truck operators under lease-to-own agreements. The sample represented $229,350 of the $47,918,615 reported total project costs. CSS' supporting records disclosed that the total reported cost for each project in the sample generally included the truck purchase price, sales taxes, repair costs, and global positioning system installation costs. CSS used the total reported cost for each project to calculate the payments specified in the lease agreement associated with the project. Our review of invoices and other available supporting records provided by CSS identified that the cost of one truck project was understated and the costs of the other three projects were overstated. Table 3 below summarizes the results of our review.

Table 3: Comparison of reported project costs with supporting records

Project	Reported cost	Supported costs	Difference
PHA -007	$25,925	$26,841	($916)
JBC028	26,816	26,733	83
P1B102-103	93,128	91,855	1,273
P1B102-331	83,481	83,012	469
Total	$229,350	$228,441	$909

Source: Invoices, lease documents, and other supporting documents provided by CSS.

As a result, payments established under leases for these four projects were based on either understated or overstated project costs. We did not expand the scope of our testing for reported project costs and lease payments because CSS had not implemented a project cost system for expenditures under the CA-funded revolving loan fund program as discussed earlier in this chapter. Therefore, we were not able to verify whether reported project costs were allocable to the CA.

CSS management acknowledged that project costs could not be reconciled to supporting records and said that the costs for each project included estimated rather than actual repair costs. According to CSS management, CSS was required to estimate the total cost of each project for the following reasons:

- CSS was required to provide potential lessees with the price of the trucks prior to ordering the vehicles shipped; therefore, CSS was unable to determine the repair costs associated with the vehicles until they arrived.
- CSS ordered trucks in batches and repaired them in batches.
- The costs associated with repairing the trucks were billed monthly to CSS and not broken down by individual trucks.

CSS management also stated that the estimated allowance for repairs averages out over time, and CSS adjusts the estimate according to the projects and anticipated repairs.

Title 2 CFR Part 230, Appendix A, A.2 (a) and (g), require costs to be allocable and adequately documented to be considered allowable under an award. In addition, 40 CFR Part 30.21(b)(2) requires recipients' financial management systems to include records that adequately identify the source and application of funds for federally sponsored activities. This regulation further states that these records should include information pertaining to assets, outlays, income, and interest. CSS was unable to support that all reported projects costs are allowable under 2 CFR Part 230 and 40 CFR Part 30. CSS was also unable to accurately identify income or losses from leases or measure whether leases and the revolving fund program were economically sound because it did not meet the financial management requirements of 40 CFR Part 30.

Progress Reporting Not Accurate

CSS' progress report for the quarter ending December 2010 did not accurately identify expenditures by funding source, the number of projects, and the total cost of projects in the revolving fund program.

Programmatic Condition 5 of the CA requires CSS to provide EPA with quarterly reports that address progress toward achieving the work plan goals. The condition specifies that the reports will include summary information on planned activities, implementation of diesel emission reduction strategies, expenditures, and issuance of loans, leases, or bonds.

Our review of CSS records associated with revolving fund activities identified that the organization's progress report for the quarter ending December 31, 2010, submitted to EPA was not accurate. The report disclosed that CSS spent $8,982,000 of CA funding on revolving fund projects. However, CSS' records showed that reported funding amounts for expenditures on projects partially funded through both CA and financial institution loan funding were not correct. According to CSS records, the recipient overstated EPA and understated financial institution-funded expenditures for projects listed in the quarterly report. We discussed this issue with CSS staff and management in March 2011. In response, in May 2011, CSS provided us with revised report information covering the quarter ending December 31, 2010. A comparison of the report submitted to EPA with the revised information showed that the quarterly report overstated CA-funded expenditures by $5,458,808 and understated expenditures funded through financial institution loans by $5,354,928. The comparison also identified that the number of projects was overstated and total project costs and funding from other sources were understated in the quarterly report. The differences between the quarterly report and the revised information are summarized in table 4 below.

Table 4: Comparison of quarterly report with corrected information

Report Category	Quarterly report for period ending December 2010	Revised report information	Difference
Number of projects	798	759	39
Total project costs	$47,918,615	$48,531,668	($613,053)
Down payments on projects	$695,969	$904,658	($208,689)
State grant-funded Expenditures	$20,099,849	$20,220,703	($120,854)
Expenditures funded by financial institution loans	$18,140,796	$23,495,724	($5,354,928)
CA-funded expenditures	$8,982,000	$3,523,192	$5,458,808

Source: CSS progress report for quarter ending December 2010 and updated program reporting information covering the reporting period.

Our review of the revised report information also identified that CSS has $777,545 of EPA funds that appear to be available to revolve to other projects. However, we were unable to verify whether the revised information was accurate because of the other financial management issues discussed earlier in the chapter. Without accurate quarterly reporting by CSS, EPA is unable to measure the recipient's progress toward achieving the goals of the CA.

Primary Cause for Financial Management Issues

We found that the financial management issues were primarily caused by CSS' underestimating accounting system requirements for the revolving fund. According to CSS management, CSS thought it could manage the revolving fund without using the limited project cost function of the accounting system. However, the management said that as the complexity of the fund increased, CSS' accounting system was not sophisticated enough to provide tracking of all sources and uses of funding. Management also said that CSS understands that improvements are needed and the organization is working to make improvements to the accounting system that will provide better visibility of the revolving fund.

Conclusion

Based on the findings above, CSS does not meet the minimum requirements for a financial management system. We are unable to provide an opinion on the financial resources, related liabilities, revenue, expenses, and residual balances of the revolving fund because of the financial management deficiencies. As a result, we question the $9 million drawn under the CA as unallowable costs under 2 CFR Part 230. Therefore, we recommend that EPA recover these questioned costs if CSS is unable to provide records that show the costs meet federal financial management requirements.

Title 2 CFR Part 180, *OMB Guidelines to Agencies on Governmentwide Debarment and Suspension (Nonprocurement)*, at subsection 180.800(b), specifies that an Agency may pursue a suspension and debarment action for violations of the terms of a public agreement or transaction so serious as to affect the integrity of an agency program. During FY 2009, EPA awarded a total of $30 million in Recovery Act funding to recipients for SmartWay Clean Diesel Finance Program projects. EPA's $9 million award to CSS represents 30 percent of the Recovery Act awards under this program. Therefore, CSS' financial management deficiencies pose a serious threat to the integrity of the Recovery Act-funded portion of EPA's Clean Diesel Finance Program. Consequently, EPA should consider suspension and debarment of CSS on current and future awards under 2 CFR Part 180.

To address the financial management issues identified during our review, CSS should establish controls to ensure that the use of funding provided under the CA complies with 40 CFR Part 30.21. These controls should ensure (1) accurate, current, and complete disclosure of the financial results of the revolving loan program; (2) records identifying the source and application of funds provided under the CA; and (3) effective control over and accountability for all funds, property, and other assets of the EPA-funded revolving loan program.

EPA should also impose special conditions on all current and future awards of EPA funds as outlined in 40 CFR Part 30. Title 40 CFR Part 30.14, *Special Award Conditions*, states:

> If an applicant or recipient: has a history of poor performance, is not financially stable; has a management system that does not meet the standards prescribed in Circular A-110; has not conformed to the terms and conditions of a previous award; or is not otherwise responsible, EPA may impose additional requirements as needed, provided that such applicant or recipient is notified in writing as to: the nature of the additional requirements, the reason why the additional requirements are being imposed, the nature of the corrective action needed, the time allowed for completing the corrective actions, and the method for requesting reconsideration of the additional requirements imposed.

The special conditions should include (1) payment on a reimbursement basis and (2) EPA review and approval of reimbursement requests prior to payment.

Recommendations

We recommend that the Director for the Office of Grants and Debarment:

1. Disallow and recover $9 million in questioned costs claimed under CA 2A-83440701. If CSS provides documentation that meets appropriate federal financial management requirements and shows that some or all of the questioned costs are allocable and allowable to the CA, the amount to be recovered should be adjusted accordingly.

2. Consider suspension and debarment of CSS on current and future awards under 2 CFR Part 180.

3. Require CSS to establish controls that ensure the use of funding provided under the CA is in compliance with 40 CFR Part 30.21. The controls should ensure:

   a. Accurate, current, and complete disclosure of the financial results of the revolving loan program funded under the CA.
   b. Records that identify adequately the source and application of funds provided under the CA.
   c. Effective control over and accountability for all funds, property, and other assets of the EPA-funded revolving loan program.

4. Require that the following special conditions be included for future EPA awards to CSS until EPA determines that the recipient has met all applicable federal financial management requirements:

   a. Payment on a reimbursement basis.
   b. Review and approval by the EPA project officer of reimbursement requests, including all supporting documentation for the claims prior to payment.

5. Provide clarifying guidance to CSS on financial and other project information required to be included in quarterly progress reports and request the recipient to submit corrected progress reports as appropriate for prior quarters of the project period.

EPA and Recipient Comments

The OIG received comments on the draft report from EPA's Office of Grants and Debarment and CSS. CSS also provided supplemental documentation as support for its comments. The supplemental documentation is not included in the report but is available upon request.

The Agency generally agreed with the accuracy of the report findings and said that it has initiated corrective actions to address some of the weaknesses identified in the draft report. The Agency explained that it changed CSS' status from advance to reimbursement payments for active assistance agreements to restrict access to available federal funds and placed a stop work order on the SmartWay Three Finance Program Agreement. The Agency noted that, in response to the CSS' 2010 single audit, the recipient acknowledged the limitations of its accounting system and indicated that significant resources have been invested to upgrade its information and accounting processes. The Agency further explained that it is imperative for EPA to determine whether CSS has made the necessary corrections in order to continue financing for the SmartWay Three Program and releasing available funding for other assistance agreements with the recipient. As a result, the Agency requested that the OIG perform a follow-up review of CSS' financial system and controls. EPA's complete written response is in appendix A.

Recommendation 5 was added after receipt of comments from EPA and CSS. EPA agreed to the recommendation and commented that, prior to the OIG's review of the CA, it provided additional guidance to CSS on reporting. EPA requested CSS provide additional project level information, including a breakdown of funding sources and an update of "Phase 2" of the cooperative agreement. EPA also reiterated the need to continue reporting on projects until the CA is closed out.

CSS disagreed with all but one of the findings and recommendation 2 in chapter 3 of the draft report. CSS neither agreed or disagreed with recommendations 1 and 3. CSS disagreed primarily because it believed that it has complied with all federal financial management requirements and shown all costs to be allocable and allowable under the CA. With regard to recommendation 4, CSS said that it concurred with a caveat that regional awards be exempt. CSS explained that the special conditions under recommendation 4 should not be placed on regional awards because these funding agreements are straightforward to administer and EPA has never had questions concerning the recipient's implementation of the awards. CSS' complete written response is in appendix B.

OIG Response

We agree with the Agency's initial corrective actions to address some of the findings and will perform the requested follow-up review of CSS' financial system and controls. The Agency will need to provide a proposed management decision for full resolution of the findings and recommendations in response to this report.

CSS' comments and supplemental documentation did not resolve the financial management issues discussed in the draft report. Therefore, our position on the findings and recommendations generally remains unchanged. We made two changes to the report based on CSS' comments. First, we revised the report to more clearly explain that we were unable to reconcile $6.7 million in draws with expenditures made under the CA both because the CA funding was recorded in general ledger accounts and deposited into bank accounts that included funds from other sources. Second, we added a recommendation that the Agency provide clarifying guidance to CSS on the content of quarterly progress reports and request the recipient to submit corrected reports as appropriate.

The full text of our response is embedded as text boxes in CSS' complete written response in appendix B.

Chapter 4
Procurements Did Not Meet Federal or Recipient Requirements

CSS' procurements under the CA did not meet federal requirements or the organization's procurement policy. Truck and emissions control equipment procurements did not meet competition or cost and price analysis requirements of 40 CFR Part 30 or CSS' procurement policy. In addition, procurements of pre-2007 model year (MY) trucks did not meet emission requirements specified by the CA. As a result, we were unable to determine whether reported total procurement costs of $8,982,000 for trucks and equipment are fair and reasonable, and pre-2007 MY trucks procured at a total cost of $1,915,918 are not allowable under the CA. We found two primary causes for the procurement issues. First, CSS staff believed that CSS followed procurement guidelines provided by the first project officer for the CA. Second, CSS had not received anticipated grant funding for retrofitting the pre-2007 MY trucks.

Procurements Did Not Meet Requirements

Truck and emission control equipment procurements did not meet requirements of 40 CFR Part 30 or CSS' procurement policy. CSS procured trucks without following a formal and documented competitive process. CSS also did not document cost or price analyses for procurements of truck emission control equipment.

Title 40 CFR Part 30 includes procurement standards that apply to the CA award. Title 40 CFR Part 30.43 requires all recipient procurement transactions to be conducted in a manner that provides, to the maximum extent practical, free and open competition. Title 40 CFR Part 30.45 also requires some form of a cost or price analysis to be made and documented in the procurement files for every procurement action. Minimum documentation requirements for purchases exceeding $100,000 are specified by 40 CFR Part 30.46. Under 40 CFR Part 30.46, the recipient's procurement records and files are required to include at a minimum the (1) basis for selection, (2) justification for lack of competition, and (3) basis for the award cost or price. Similar to 40 CFR Part 30, CSS' procurement policy requires a formal bid process and retention in the transaction records of documentation on the selection process for procurements of $50,000 or greater.

Our review of a judgmental sample of 4 of CSS' 27 completed truck procurement actions with costs exceeding $100,000 for the period September 28, 2009, through June 9, 2010, disclosed that the purchases did not meet competition and documentation requirements. The sample represented $3,303,337 million of $10,477,704 in total costs incurred for the 27 procurement actions. Supporting documents for the sample generally consisted of the invoices and payment records for the procurements. The supporting records did not include the cost or price analysis documentation specified by 40 CFR Part 30.45 or the competition and other documentation specified by 40 CFR Part 30.46 and CSS' procurement policy.

We also reviewed a judgmental sample of 11 out of 472 truck emission control equipment procurements with costs below $100,000 for the period ending December 31, 2011. The sample represented $163,193 of $4,987,923 in reported costs incurred for truck emission control equipment. CSS procured the emission equipment upgrades for trucks owned by truck operators or trucking companies. Supporting documents for the sample generally consisted of the invoices for the procurements and calculation documents showing repayment amounts for the recipients of the equipment. CSS' documentation associated with the procurements did not show that a cost or price analysis had been conducted. According to CSS management, CSS did conduct a cost or price analysis for equipment procurements, but the analysis was not documented. We did not expand the sample because of the other material deficiencies with CSS' financial management system discussed earlier in this report.

CSS' progress report for the quarter ending December 31, 2010, identified that $8,982,000 in CA funding had been spent on truck and emission control equipment procurements. We were unable to determine whether these procurement costs are fair and reasonable because CSS did not meet the procurement requirements of 40 CFR Part 30 or its internal policy.

In response to these procurement issues, CSS staff said that CSS followed procurement guidelines provided by the first project officer for the CA. As support, CSS staff provided an April 2010 e-mail from the first project officer disclosing these guidelines. The first project officer stated in the e-mail:

> …CSS' lease program allows drivers to either 1) select their vehicle from a list of eligible vehicles offered by a number of dealers or 2) present a vehicle that is eligible under CSS' program requirements. Given CSS' lease program parameters, this approach sounds reasonable in trying to ensure open competition for selecting the most appropriate vehicles. Again, all procurement transactions should provide, to the maximum extent practical, open and free competition.

The first project officer is no longer employed by EPA. Therefore, we were unable to discuss the e-mail with this project officer. However, the project officer's e-mail does not instruct CSS to ignore the cost or price analysis documentation requirement specified by 40 CFR Part 30.45, the competition and other documentation requirements specified by 40 CFR Part 30.46, or the organization's procurement policy.

Procurement of Pre-2007 Model Year Trucks Did Not Meet CA Requirements

CSS did not install emission control technologies on pre-2007 MY trucks as required by the CA. Programmatic Condition 3.1.G of the CA specifies that CSS may use the funding under the award to purchase or lease pre-2007 MY on-highway vehicles, used engines, and used pieces of equipment as long as verified emission control technologies have been installed. CSS' progress report for the quarter ending December 31, 2010, submitted to EPA, identified that $1,915,918 in CA funds were used to procure 227 pre-2007 MY trucks. The quarterly report also disclosed that these trucks had not been retrofitted with emission control technologies because CSS had not received anticipated grant funding for the retrofits from California. According to CSS staff, retrofitting the trucks may not be economically viable because the cost of the emission control equipment exceeds the value of the trucks.

The $1,915,918 in costs incurred by CSS for the pre-2007 MY trucks are not allowable under the CA because required emission control technologies have not been installed. The progress report for the quarter ending December 31, 2010 disclosed that CSS may remove the pre-2007 MY trucks from the revolving fund program and replace them with trucks that meet the CA requirements to resolve the issue. At the time of our field work, EPA was working with CSS to resolve the issue.

Recommendations

We recommend that the Director for the Office of Grants and Debarment:

6. Require CSS to comply at a minimum with 40 CFR Part 30 for past and future procurements under the CA. Specifically, require CSS to:

    a. Maintain in the procurement records the minimum documentation specified by 40 CFR Part 30.46 for procurements exceeding $100,000.
    b. Conduct and maintain in the procurement records a cost or price analysis for every procurement action as required by 40 CFR Part 30.45.

7. Disallow the pre-2007 MY trucks as project costs under the EPA-funded revolving loan program unless CSS provides EPA with documentation verifying that the trucks have been retrofitted with emission control devices as specified by the CA.

EPA and Recipient Comments

The OIG received comments on the draft report from EPA's Office of Grants and Debarment and CSS. CSS also provided supplemental documentation as support for its comments. The supplemental documentation is not included in the report but is available upon request.

The Agency generally agreed with the accuracy of the findings of the report and said that it has initiated corrective actions to address some of the weaknesses identified in the draft report.

CSS acknowledged that it did not comply with applicable procurement requirements for both truck and equipment expenditures. CSS said that it did not comply because it did not believe the requirements were applicable. CSS explained that it does not consider itself as the procurer but rather an agent acting on behalf of its customers who select the trucks and equipment for purchase. CSS said that it now understands that the OIG and EPA consider its truck and equipment expenditures to be subject to the procurement requirements of 40 CFR Part 30. With regard to the pre-2007 MY trucks, CSS said that the retrofits were significantly delayed because it did not receive anticipated California Air Resources Board funding for the emission control equipment.

CSS did not specifically state whether it agreed with recommendation 6, but CSS' comments indicate concurrence. CSS said that it retroactively complied with EPA's procurement requirements and included documentation presenting the results with its response to the draft report. CSS also said that, in the future, it will maintain the minimum required documentation for procurements exceeding $100,000 and conduct a cost or price analysis for every procurement action.

CSS strongly disagreed with recommendation 7. CSS said the EPA project officer expressly approved the purchase of the pre-2007 MY trucks with the condition that the trucks would be retrofitted at a later date. CSS also said that it is in the process of retrofitting the trucks, and the retrofits will be completed by June 17, 2012.

CSS' complete written response is in appendix B.

OIG Response

We agree with the Agency's initial corrective actions to address some of the findings in the draft report. The Agency will need to provide a proposed management decision for full resolution of the findings and recommendations in response to this report.

CSS' comments and supplemental documentation did not resolve the procurement issues discussed in the draft report. Therefore, our position on the findings and recommendations remains unchanged. With regard to CSS' comment that it retroactively complied with EPA's procurement requirements for past procurements, we were unable to verify whether the corrective actions satisfactorily resolve the documentation and analyses issues because sufficient information and supporting documentation was not included in the response to the draft report. CSS' current plan to retrofit the pre-2007 MY trucks by June 2012 will not achieve emissions standards over the long-term. According to CSS, the retrofits provide emission control equipment that is only valid for approximately 6 months. As a result, expenditures for the pre-2007 MY trucks do not represent effective and efficient use of Recovery Act funds and are not reasonable costs under the CA.

The full text of our response is embedded as text boxes in CSS' complete written response in appendix B.

Chapter 5
Job Reporting Does Not Comply With OMB Guidance

CSS' reporting of jobs created or retained with Recovery Act funds did not comply with OMB reporting guidance. The Recovery Act requires quarterly reporting for the number of jobs created and retained with Recovery Act funding. OMB guidance on Recovery Act quarterly reporting requirements specifies that the estimated total number of jobs funded is to be reported by recipients. The guidance also specifies that information should be collected from all subrecipients and vendors, to the maximum extent possible, to generate the most comprehensive and complete job impact numbers available. CSS incorrectly calculated the number of jobs created or retained for quarterly reports covering the period October 2009 through June 2010 by including in its computations (1) CSS labor hours funded with income from the revolving fund program and (2) full-time equivalent (FTE) positions of truck operators for trucks procured by CSS with Recovery Act funding and subsequently leased to the operators.

Under the OMB reporting guidance, CSS labor hours should not have been included in the computation of the number of jobs created or retained because they were not funded through the Recovery Act. The FTE truck operator positions should not have been included in the computation because the operators for the leased trucks are beneficiaries rather than recipients or subrecipients of Recovery Act funding. As a result, CSS overstated the number of jobs created or retained with Recovery Act funds during the period October 2009 through June 2010. For example, we found that CSS overstated the number of jobs created or retained by 79 FTE for the quarter ended December 31, 2009.

According to CSS staff involved in Recovery Act reporting, the number of jobs CSS reported as created or retained was based on guidance provided by the EPA project officer for the CA award. The CSS staff said that the first EPA project officer for the award agreed with CSS' reporting methodology. The staff explained that the project officer's rationale for agreeing to the methodology was that (1) income from the revolving loan program was the result of Recovery Act funding, and (2) FTE positions of operators for trucks leased by CSS capture the essence of jobs retained as a result of Recovery Act funding. We were unable to confirm whether EPA agreed to or approved CSS' reporting methodology because the first project officer for the award is no longer employed by EPA. Neither the current project officer nor EPA management associated with the award were aware of the first project officer's guidance on Recovery Act reporting provided to CSS.

OMB's Recovery Act guidance requires that recipients of Recovery Act funding maintain corrections to erroneous and missing data submitted in prior quarterly reports in their administrative records. The guidance also requires that recipients submit the corrections to the federal government at a time to be specified in the future.

Recommendations

We recommend that the Director for the Office of Grants and Debarment:

8. Assist CSS with developing a methodology for calculating the number of jobs created or retained for quarterly reports that meets OMB guidance on Recovery Act reporting.

9. Direct CSS to correct the number of jobs created or retained in the quarterly reports covering the period October 1, 2009, to June 30, 2010, and all subsequent periods with job reporting errors, to comply with OMB guidance on Recovery Act reporting.

10. Direct CSS to maintain the corrected jobs documentation referenced in recommendation 8 in the administrative records and submit the corrections to the federal government after a schedule has been established by future Recovery Act guidance.

EPA and Recipient Comments

The OIG received comments on the draft report from EPA's Office of Grants and Debarment and CSS. The Agency generally agreed with the accuracy of the findings and said that it has initiated corrective actions to address some of the weaknesses identified in the draft report. However, CSS disagreed with the findings and said that it had followed EPA's methodology and guidance on reporting the number of jobs created or retained with Recovery Act funds. CSS explained that the EPA program office had agreed to its methodology after the recipient had proactively sought guidance from EPA on Recovery Act reporting. CSS also said that it believed the methodology it was using was appropriate and correct because EPA was approving the quarterly Recovery Act reports.

Although CSS disagreed with the findings, the recipient said it stands ready to collaborate with EPA to implement the recommendations. CSS' complete written response is in appendix B.

OIG Response

We agree with the Agency's initial corrective actions to address some of the findings in the draft report. The Agency will need to provide a proposed management decision for full resolution of the findings and recommendations in response to this report.

CSS' comments did not resolve the Recovery Act reporting issues discussed in the draft report. We were unable to confirm whether EPA agreed with CSS' reporting methodology because the first project officer is no longer employed by the EPA as discussed in the draft report. With regard to CSS' comment on EPA's approval of its Recovery Act reports, EPA staff did not verify that the number of jobs created or retained in the reports were correct and met the OMB guidance on Recovery Act quarterly reporting. Therefore, our position on the findings and recommendations remains unchanged.

We agree that CSS should collaborate with EPA to implement the recommendations. The full text of our response is embedded as text boxes in CSS' complete written response in appendix B.

Status of Recommendations and Potential Monetary Benefits

| | | RECOMMENDATIONS | | | | POTENTIAL MONETARY BENEFITS (in $000s) | |
Rec. No.	Page No.	Subject	Status[1]	Action Official	Planned Completion Date	Claimed Amount	Agreed To Amount
1	13	Disallow and recover $9 million in questioned costs claimed under CA 2A-83440701. If CSS provides documentation that meets appropriate federal financial management requirements and shows that some or all of the questioned costs are allocable and allowable to the CA, the amount to be recovered should be adjusted accordingly.	U	Director, Office of Grants and Debarment		$9,000	
2	13	Consider suspension and debarment of CSS on current and future awards under 2 CFR Part 180.	U	Director, Office of Grants and Debarment			
3	13	Require CSS to establish controls that ensure the use of funding provided under the CA is in compliance with 40 CFR Part 30.21. The controls should ensure: a. Accurate, current, and complete disclosure of the financial results of the revolving loan program funded under the CA. b. Records that identify adequately the source and application of funds provided under the CA. c. Effective control over and accountability for all funds, property, and other assets of the EPA-funded revolving loan program.	U	Director, Office of Grants and Debarment			
4	14	Require that the following special conditions be included for future EPA awards to CSS until EPA determines that the recipient has met all applicable federal financial management requirements: a. Payment on a reimbursement basis. b. Review and approval by EPA project officer of reimbursement requests, including all supporting documentation for the claims prior to payment.	U	Director, Office of Grants and Debarment			
5	14	Provide clarifying guidance to CSS on financial and other project information required to be included in quarterly progress reports and request the recipient to submit corrected progress reports as appropriate for prior quarters of the project period.	U	Director, Office of Grants and Debarment			
6	18	Require CSS to comply at a minimum with 40 CFR Part 30 for past and future procurements under the CA. Specifically, require CSS to: a. Maintain in the procurement records the minimum documentation specified by 40 CFR Part 30.46 for procurements exceeding $100,000. b. Conduct and maintain in the procurement records a cost or price analysis for every procurement action as required by 40 CFR Part 30.45.	U	Director, Office of Grants and Debarment			

Rec. No.	Page No.	Subject	Status[1]	Action Official	Planned Completion Date	Claimed Amount	Agreed To Amount
7	18	Disallow the pre-2007 MY trucks as project costs under the EPA-funded revolving loan program unless CSS provides EPA with documentation verifying that the trucks have been retrofitted with emission control devices as specified by the CA.	U	Director, Office of Grants and Debarment			
8	22	Assist CSS with developing a methodology for calculating the number of jobs created or retained for quarterly reports that meets OMB guidance on Recovery Act reporting.	U	Director, Office of Grants and Debarment			
9	22	Direct CSS to correct the number of jobs created or retained in the quarterly reports covering the period October 1, 2009, to June 30, 2010, and all subsequent periods with job reporting errors, to comply with OMB guidance on Recovery Act reporting.	U	Director, Office of Grants and Debarment			
10	22	Direct CSS to maintain the corrected jobs documentation referenced in recommendation 8 in the administrative records and submit the corrections to the federal government after a schedule has been established by future Recovery Act guidance.	U	Director, Office of Grants and Debarment			

[1] O = recommendation is open with agreed-to corrective actions pending
    C = recommendation is closed with all agreed-to actions completed
    U = recommendation is unresolved with resolution efforts in progress

Agency's Comments on Draft Report

UNITED STATES ENVIRONMENTAL PROTECTION AGENCY
WASHINGTON, D.C. 20460

OFFICE OF
ADMTNISTRATION
AND RESOURCES
MANAGEMENT

February 3, 2012

MEMORANDUM

SUBJECT: Comments on Draft Attestation Report, "Examination of Costs Claimed Under EPA Cooperative Agreement 2A-83440701 Awarded Under the Recovery Act to Cascade Sierra Solutions" Project No. OA-FY11-A-0062

FROM: Howard Corcoran, Director
Office of Grants and Debarment

TO: Robert Adachi, Director
Forensic Audits

Thank you for the opportunity to review and comment on the factual accuracy of the subject Office of Inspector General Draft Attestation Report dated December 20, 2011. We sincerely appreciate your prompt and comprehensive examination of this matter. Based on our review of the Draft Report and information available at this time, we generally agree with the accuracy of the findings in the Report.

The agency has initiated corrective actions to address some of the weaknesses identified in the Draft Report. The agency has placed CSS on reimbursement status for the active assistance agreements to restrict access to available federal funds.

In addition, the agency has placed a stop work order for the Smartway Three Finance Program Agreement DE-83469401, until CSS can demonstrate that their financial system can effectively record and report the source and application of funds associated with the grant project.

In response to their 2010 single audit, CSS acknowledged the limitations of their accounting system identified in that report and indicated that they have invested significant resources to upgrade their information and accounting processes, including an integrated database system that will provide the additional reporting capabilities they need. CSS responded that they have added staff and provided training to improve their recording, tracking and reporting capabilities of their lease and loan programs. In addition, CSS responded in their single audit that they have created a Grant Compliance Department to implement the internal controls needed to manage and document their assistance agreement activities. In a November, 2011 meeting, CSS reiterated these improvements to the agency.

At present, the agency is unable to determine if the OIG fieldwork for its draft report takes into account the improvements that CSS has reportedly made in response to their single audit. Many of the weaknesses and corrective actions identified in the 2010 CSS single audit are similar to those identified in the OIG Draft Report.

In order to continue with financing the Smartway Three Program as well as release existing available funds for other headquarters assistance agreements with CSS, it is imperative that the agency determine whether CSS has made these necessary corrections to their financial systems and organization and whether the improvements are effective in correcting the weaknesses identified going forward.

Accordingly, the agency respectfully requests that the OIG perform a follow up review of CSS' financial systems and controls. The OIG is best equipped to perform this assessment since it conducted the onsite review identifying the weaknesses in CSS' financial systems and therefore would be in a position to more quickly determine whether CSS has corrected the system weaknesses. The intent of the follow up review would be to assess if CSS' financial system can adequately:

- Provide a current and complete disclosure of the financial results of CSS' assistance agreements with the agency;
- Identify the source and application of grant funds; and
- Provide control over all funds, property and assets associated with EPA assistance agreements.

By obtaining this information the agency will be able to determine whether the EPA should continue its Smartway assistance agreements with CSS.

Thank you once again for the opportunity to comment on the Draft Report and for your review of the recipient's claimed costs. If you have any questions concerning this matter, please feel free to contact Joe Lucia, the Office of Grants and Debarment's assistance agreement Audit Follow-up Coordinator. You may reach Joe by email at lucia.joseph@epa.gov, or by phone at 202-564-5378.

cc: Nanci Gelb
        Wendel Askew
        Don Flattery
        Gayle Jefferson
        Denise Sirmons
        Phil Schindel
        Kysha Holliday
        Joe Lucia
        Carl Davis
        Jessica Durand
        Tyler Cooley
        Rosalva Tapia

CSS's Comments on the Draft Report and OIG Evaluation

The response from CSS is provided verbatim. OIG responses to those comments have been inserted in text boxes.

**Examination of Costs Claimed
Under EPA Cooperative Agreement 2A-83440701
Awarded Under the Recovery Act
to Cascade Sierra Solutions**

Project No. OA-FY11-A-0062

Response of Cascade Sierra Solutions

February 21, 2012

Examination of Costs Claimed Under EPA Cooperative Agreement 2A-83440701 Awarded Under the Recovery Act to Cascade Sierra Solutions, Project No. OA-FY11-A-0062

Comments of Cascade Sierra Solutions

I.   Introduction

Cascade Sierra Solutions (CSS) appreciates the opportunity to submit these comments on the Environmental Protection Agency (EPA) Office of Inspector General's (OIG) Draft Examination of Cost Claimed Under EPA Cooperative Agreement 2A-83440701 Awarded Under the Recovery Act to Cascade Sierra Solutions (OIG Draft Report). Cooperative Agreement 2A-83440701 (the CA), which was CSS's second award under EPA's National SmartWay Finance Program (SWFP), awarded $9 million to CSS under the American Reinvestment and Recovery Act of 2009 (ARRA or the Recovery Act) for the purpose of creating a national revolving loan program for heavy-duty diesel trucks to save fuel and reduce diesel emissions. The CA project period originally covered June 1, 2009 to October 31, 2011, but has been extended by EPA through October 31, 2012. OIG's audit of CSS commenced on March 7, 2011 and was conducted for the purpose of determining whether CSS complied with the terms of the CA, ARRA, and applicable EPA and OMB regulations.

CSS takes its responsibility to comply with all applicable federal requirements very seriously and thus finds the OIG Draft Report's results to be very troubling. Because of this, CSS has communicated with EPA about the audit's findings and an appropriate response to the audit. For this reason, CSS, in this document, responds comprehensively to the issues raised by the audit.

II.   Cascade Sierra Solutions and EPA

CSS has an extensive relationship with the EPA SmartWay Program because its focus on promoting the use of EPA SmartWay Verified Technologies to save diesel fuel and reduce diesel emissions strongly aligns with the mission of EPA's Clean Diesel Program. The CA that is the subject of this audit is only one of several grants that CSS has been awarded by EPA. At present, in addition to the CA, CSS administers six other SmartWay awards—two other active SmartWay National Finance Program Awards, which help implement the revolving loan fund, and four other regional SmartWay awards, under which CSS provides incentives for the installation of emission control equipment and fuel saving technologies.[1] All told, under its ten past and active SmartWay awards, CSS has successfully administered over $15.7 million in EPA funds.

CSS is a leader in modernizing the American heavy-duty diesel fleet. As a not-for-profit organization dedicated to lending money to Independent Owner Operators who do not have ready access to credit, CSS is playing a crucial role in modernizing the heavy-duty diesel fleet that is not replicated elsewhere in the U.S. CSS' mission and focus on modernizing the diesel fleet is critical because of its wide-ranging effects: it improves air quality and public health, reduces American dependence on foreign oil, and creates jobs for small- and minority-owned businesses.

Because of its success, CSS is a bright light in EPA's SmartWay Program and national efforts to reduce diesel emissions. In less than five years, CSS has retrofitted more than 7,000 vehicles across the nation to improve their fuel efficiency and reduce the harmful exhaust emissions they produce. The retrofitted vehicles now save more than 30,000 gallons of diesel fuel per day and have collectively saved over 35 million gallons to date. Each retrofitted vehicle will, on average, over the course of its lifetime, reduce its emissions of CO_2 by 350 metric tons, particulate matter by 289 pounds, and NO_x by 5,000 pounds, and eliminate $12,500 in health care costs that would otherwise be incurred because of air pollution. CSS is not merely adding cleaner vehicles to the fleet; CSS is transforming the fleet. Because of its revolving loan fund, CSS has already removed thousands of old, fuel-inefficient, and polluting vehicles that would have remained on American roadways for up to 25 years each, and as the fund revolves, more benefits continue to accrue.

CSS' success particularly stands out because of the results that CSS has achieved within the SmartWay program. As the only three-time recipient of a SmartWay Finance Award, CSS has, by far, put more clean trucks on the nation's roads than any of the other SmartWay Finance participants. To CSS' knowledge, CSS has reduced more emissions than any other organization participating in the SmartWay Finance Program. Further, CSS has achieved its results over a very short time period and against the backdrop of a difficult national economy. With respect to the CA, which was granted under ARRA to stimulate the national economy, CSS deployed the majority of the $9 million in CA funds to eligible projects within three months of receipt of those funds. CSS has delivered impressive results under challenging circumstances.

CSS' outstanding results are possible because of the innovative nature of CSS' revolving loan fund, which utilizes a model that leverages federal dollars by up to a 16-to-1 ratio with private sector dollars. In a time of reduced government budgets, the CSS public-private revolving loan fund program is a model for the future, and should not be criticized because it breaks the mold of government accounting regulations.

CSS' revolving loan fund program, funded by the CA, is the first of its kind. CSS has achieved great success because of its unique and innovative public-private revolving loan fund

---

[1] The SmartWay Finance Awards are Award Nos. DE-83412001 and DE-83469401, and the Regional Awards are Award Nos. 2A-96114901 (Region 1), 2A-97232501 (Region 2), DE-00F11201 (Region 6), and DE-00J606801 (Region 10).

model. Because the trucking industry is a high-risk industry, many financial institutions are unwilling to provide financing to Independent Owner Operators (IOOs) or small fleets, and thus, significant barriers to capital exist. CSS sought to break down this barrier in the credit markets by developing a revolving loan program that finances SmartWay-eligible equipment for IOOs and small fleets. The CSS revolving loan fund overcomes the market's inability to provide financing to these borrowers by utilizing EPA funds to mitigate the credit risk associated with financing eligible truck replacement and after-market upgrade projects, thereby encouraging private lenders to participate in the market for small trucking businesses.

CSS knows of no other program that pairs public and private money through a revolving loan fund that multiplies the effect of federal dollars and continually replenishes itself. Because of the leveraging of private sector funds, the CSS model is unlike that used by EPA under the Clean Water Act Revolving Fund. After only a very short period of implementation of the CSS revolving loan fund, both CSS and the EPA Program Office agreed that the public-private revolving loan fund model is a very efficient use of government resources that represents a new and better way to implement public-private partnerships.

However, CSS' success has not come without struggles and hard work. Although CSS has gotten the revolving loan fund model to function sustainably—it now has several lenders that actively participate in making CSS loans on an ongoing basis—CSS has found it challenging to fit its revolving loan fund program into EPA's existing grant regulations. For instance, the design of the CSS revolving loan fund, as proposed to EPA, blends public and private dollars in individual financing agreements, and does not rely on traditional segregation of fund principles. Also, the subordination of EPA funds to private sector funding initially raised questions concerning the Federal Government's property standards. Through discussion with CSS, EPA Program Administrators addressed these issues within CSS' third SmartWay Finance (SW3) award and amended the SW3 agreement as necessary. The development of the SmartWay Finance program began when EPA Program Administrators approached CSS regarding the success of the Everybody Wins equipment leasing program and consulted with CSS on the development of the SmartWay Finance program. In acknowledgement of these challenges, and the fact that CSS is the first public-private revolving loan fund that EPA has overseen, CSS has invested substantial time and energy in consulting with EPA regarding how to best implement its model.

In demonstrating the Everybody Wins program, and in consulting on the development of the SmartWay Finance program, CSS and EPA reached agreement on the concept of the blended loan. By blending EPA grant funds with loans from private financial institutions and grants from states and private sources, CSS maximizes the cost effectiveness of EPA funds. This approach was clearly outlined in CSS' original proposal for the CA and the SWFP. Customer payments repay the financial institution's portion of the loan, and the remaining funds are returned to the revolving loan fund to finance additional projects.

CSS has grown rapidly as an organization. Although CSS currently funds approximately $20 million in loans per year, it is quite young as an organization. CSS was founded five years ago, in November of 2006 as a one-employee organization. After a year, CSS had grown to 10 employees, and now CSS has 57 employees.

While CSS' rapid growth has increased its capacity to finance clean diesel vehicles and equipment—CSS has now impacted close to 20,000 heavy-duty diesel trucks on the road in the United States, and plans to do much more—its success has created challenges as well. In order to keep pace with its steady growth, CSS has had to upgrade its accounting and administrative databases several times over the past five years. These upgrades have been necessary, but have at times resulted in delays and required a significant investment of time and administrative resources to implement. While CSS strongly believes that it has complied with its SmartWay grant obligations, these technological upgrades have provided an extra set of logistical challenges for an organization that operates on very limited resources.

CSS has done, and will continue to do, whatever it takes to makes its program successful, accountable, and an effective use of taxpayer dollars. Because CSS takes the OIG Draft Report seriously and values its relationship with EPA's Program and Grants offices, CSS will respond to each point raised in the Draft Report, account for all of the grant dollars it was awarded, and explain in detail the upgrades it has made to track funding and payments and address the concerns raised in the OIG Draft Report. These upgrades have come as a result of taking recommendations from prior CSS outside auditor reports and numerous discussions between CSS and EPA staff.

III. Comments on Chapter 3 – Financial Management System

A. Cash Draws Exceeded Cash Needs

The OIG Draft Report states that CSS cash draws exceeded its immediate cash needs in violation of Title 40 CFR 30.22(b)'s requirement that cash advances be limited to the minimum amounts needed and be timed to be in accordance with actual, immediate cash requirements.

CSS disagrees that its possession of advance funds in 2009 constituted draws in excess of its immediate needs in violation of Title 40 CFR 30.22. While CSS did have a large amount of advance funds in its accounts during 2009, that situation was entirely unavoidable for a number of reasons.

First, CSS needed advance funds to complete SmartWay projects at the time. In 2009, CSS did not have sufficient working capital to pre-fund CA projects, and so it requested funds for CA transactions in advance.

Second, CSS had to take into consideration EPA's turnaround time for processing draw requests under the CA when coordinating several large transactions that CSS entered into with truck wholesalers in October and November of 2009. This meant that CSS had no choice but to request the CA funds well in advance of the transactions. For instance, CSS submitted a draw request for $742,000 on October 7, 2009, and another for $1 million on October 20, 2009, but EPA did not release the funds to CSS until October 13, 2009, and October 30, 2009, respectively – six and ten days later. CSS planned to use the funds it drew down to purchase trucks from a vendor that required CSS to pay for the trucks within two weeks of inspection of the trucks.

However, after CSS drew down the advance funds to complete the transaction, the vendor delayed the inspection date repeatedly without giving CSS advance notice, which delayed the payment. However, CSS could not forgo the transaction and return the advance funds to EPA, because it had already placed a $100,000 nonrefundable deposit down on the trucks. The combination of a short payment window by several vendors, unforeseen delays, and nonrefundable deposits meant that CSS did not return the advance funds to EPA. Thus, although CSS was maintaining large amounts of CA funds on hand for a prolonged period of several weeks, it was necessary to complete several large transactions.

Third, at the time of these transactions, CSS did not have access to EPA's Automated Standard Application for Payments (ASAP) system. Access to the ASAP system would have eliminated CSS' need to have advance funds on hand for these large truck purchases, because the ASAP system reduced EPA's draw turnaround time to three days. When CSS began using the ASAP system in November 2009, the advance CA funds that it maintained on hand dropped dramatically, and by the end of December 2009, the balance of advance funds that CSS maintained on hand dropped to zero. However, while conducting a number of large truck purchases in October 2009 and early November 2009, the ASAP system was not available to CSS, so CSS was required to maintain advance funds on hand.

CSS recognized at the time that maintaining a large amount of advance CA funds in its accounts was problematic and actively consulted EPA about resolving the issue. When CSS raised the issue with its EPA Project Officer, the project officer advised CSS to obtain access to the ASAP system, which CSS immediately did. CSS also disclosed the situation to CSS' independent auditors to ensure that they found its use of advance funds to be appropriate.

i. Subsequent CSS Actions

As the OIG Draft Report stated, CSS repaid EPA $1,751 for interest the CA funds earned while present in CSS accounts. CSS understands this, together with CSS' enrollment in the ASAP system, to have satisfactorily resolved this issue, and therefore CSS has not taken further action.

OIG Response 1. Our position remains unchanged. Regardless of the issues that led to the excess cash on hand, CSS' cash draws exceeded immediate needs by as much as $3,141,127. As stated in the report, 40 CFR Part 30.22(b) specifies that cash advances are limited to the minimum amounts needed and are to be timed in accordance with the actual, immediate cash requirements of the recipient. Title 40 CFR Part 30.22(b) also specifies that the timing and amount of cash advances shall be as close as is administratively feasible to the actual disbursement by the recipient. As acknowledged in the report, CSS satisfactorily resolved the issue by remitting interest earned in excess of $250 to EPA in accordance with 40 Part 30.22(l). Our report did not recommend any further actions by CSS or EPA.

B. Cash Draws Not Supported as Allocable and Allowable

The OIG Draft Report states that CSS' cash draws were not supported by expenditures under the CA that were allocable and allowable. Noting that CSS must maintain documentation that adequately identifies the source and application of CA funds, and that CSS must track CA funds separately from other funds, the OIG Draft Report finds CSS' documentation to be inadequate for two reasons. First, it states that the commingling of CA and non-CA funds is impermissible: "[b]ecause the CA funding was deposited into accounts that included funds from other sources, we were unable to reconcile . . . deposits with expenditures made under the CA." Second, the Draft Report OIG claims that CSS documentation is inadequate because "documentation and [accounting system entries] did not include notations or coding showing that the costs were incurred under the CA." CSS respectfully disagrees with both rationales.

i. The Commingling of Funds

CSS disagrees strongly with OIG's assertion that CA funds may not be commingled with non-CA funds, and that such activity means that CSS' records are not adequate. EPA expressly approved such commingling by CSS, and nothing in the CA or EPA or OMB regulations prohibits CSS from doing so. Further, the commingling of funds is an important part of the CSS business model, and does not prohibit CSS from adequately tracking CA funds or identifying their source and application.

First, CSS submitted in its proposal, and EPA expressly approved, an arrangement in which CSS commingles CA and non-CA funds. The CA work plan that EPA approved plainly describes this idea with an example of a blended loan comprised of CA and non-CA funds: "The average purchase price of these new, clean vehicles is $120,000 each, significantly less than retail market value. Prop 1B grants will pay $50,000 and EPA SmartWay finance funds will pay the remaining $70,000."[2] Further, CA Programmatic Condition 12.4 states that "[l]oans funded in whole or in part with direct funding from EPA or program income are subject to these Terms and Conditions, even if the loan is funded in part by a non-federal source."[3] Thus, the commingling of CA and non-CA funds was undertaken only after consultation with and the express approval of EPA.[4]

Second, CSS does not find any authority in the CA, ARRA, or EPA or OMB regulations that requires it to segregate CA funds from non-CA funds. While EPA's regulations permit EPA to require the segregation of advance funds,[5] EPA did not avail itself of that option by inserting

---

[2] CA Revised Work Plan, p.3.

[3] CA, Programmatic Condition 12.4.

[4] Further, EPA's grant disbursement process requires that funds for each of CSS' regional and national grants be deposited in the same account, which unavoidably commingles CA and non-CA funds. Although CSS has established separate bank accounts for different kinds of EPA deposits, the EPA Payment Management System and the ASAP program maintain a single CSS bank account on file in which all draw requests for each of CSS' six active grants are deposited.

[5] Title 40 CFR Part 30.22(i)(1) states that "[e]xcept for situations [involving advances of federal funds], EPA shall not require separate depository accounts for funds provided to a recipient or establish any eligibility requirements for depositories for funds provided to a recipient."

any segregation requirement into the CA. Even if EPA had required CSS to segregate advance CA funds from other funds, EPA's regulations expressly prohibit EPA from requiring CSS to segregate non-advance CA funds, such as revolved loan funds and program income.[6] Neither ARRA, nor OMB regulations, directly address the question of whether CA and non-CA funds may be commingled. CSS views the fact that EPA regulations expressly address the commingling of funds, combined with the EPA Program Office's approval of CSS' commingling, to mean that EPA does not require CSS to completely segregate CA funds in order to maintain adequate documentation of CA funds.

Third, the ability to commingle funds has allowed CSS to use the CA funds in the most cost-effective manner possible. Because CSS expressly stated in its workplan, and independently to EPA, that it desires to stretch the CA funds as much as possible by using them in conjunction with other funds, CSS frequently uses CA funds and non-CA funds for the same transaction. If CSS is required to segregate all CSS funds, CSS would be required to maintain three sets of accounting and financial records in order to continue to operate as it has—one for CA funds, one for non-CA funds, and another for the combined transaction. This would reduce efficiency, drive up the administrative costs associated with loans, and correspondingly increase the burden placed on CSS employees.

OIG Response 2. We agree that nothing in the CA or applicable federal regulations prohibits CSS from commingling CA funds with other funding included in the revolving loan program. We also acknowledge that the draft report did not clearly explain the issue with the $6.7 million in deposits of CA funds to bank accounts that included funds from other sources. Based on CSS' comments, the report was revised to more clearly explain that we were unable to reconcile the $6.7 million in draws with expenditures made under the CA because the CA funding was recorded in general ledger accounts and deposited into bank accounts that included funds from other sources.

However, we disagree with CSS' comment that segregating CA and other funding for the revolving loan program would require the recipient to maintain three sets of accounting and financial records in order to continue to operate the program. Title 40 CFR Part 30.21(b)(2) specifies that recipients' financial management systems shall provide records that identify adequately the source and application of funds for federally sponsored activities. To meet this requirement, CSS will need to establish one comprehensive set of general ledger accounts for the revolving fund. As discussed in the draft report, CSS has not established this account structure in the general ledger for the revolving loan fund.

Fourth, the commingling of CA funds with non-CA funds does not prevent CSS from adequately tracking separately or identifying the source and application of CA funds. CSS SmartWay Finance awards, including the CA, have been audited multiple times by CSS' independent Certified Public Accountant, reviewed by EPA project officers and program staff, and examined under an EPA-contracted limited scope audit. CSS has provided each set of auditors with the same documentation, which included a full listing of the cash disbursements for the initial $9 million, which is reproduced in Appendix A, and documentation supporting CSS'

---

[6] *Id.*

cash advance requests and management procedures. None of CSS' auditors has claimed that CSS' commingling of funds has been problematic, or has found that CSS has failed to track separately or adequately identify the source and application of CA funds.

For instance, CSS' most recent single audit found that "Cascade Sierra Solutions complied, in all material respects, with the compliance requirements referred to above that could have a direct and material effect on each of its major federal programs for the year ended December 31, 2010," and that the auditor "did not identify any deficiencies in internal control over financial reporting that [it] consider[s] to be material weaknesses."[7] Given approval in the past for this approach by EPA and CSS auditors, CSS sees no reason why it should not be permitted to continue commingling CA and non-CA funds for the few remaining months of the CA project period.

OIG Response 3. We disagree that CSS has adequately tracked CA funds separately from other grant programs or identified the source and application of CA funds under the recipient's current financial management system. As discussed in the report, CSS' financial management system does not adequately separate the funds and assets accrued as a result of the CA. Consequently, we are unable to verify that these funds and assets are being used in accordance with the terms and conditions of the CA. We acknowledge that CSS has been previously audited by an independent Certified Public Accountant, reviewed by the EPA project officer and program staff, and examined under an EPA-contracted limited scope audit. However, these reviews either identified deficiencies similar to issues identified in our report or were more limited in scope than our examination of CSS' financial management of EPA funding received under the CA.

Regarding the single audit for the year ended December 31, 2010, the report on this single audit provided an opinion of the overall financial position of CSS and did not specifically discuss the financial position of the revolving loan program partly funded by the CA. This single audit identified five significant deficiencies in internal controls over financial reporting and two significant deficiencies in internal controls over compliance. The findings included deficient internal controls over general journal preparation, documentation, and review and approval, resulting in little or no audit trail for adjustments made by CSS. The single audit noted that the possibility existed that erroneous or unauthorized journal entries could be posted to the general ledger and not be detected. The single audit also found deficiencies in internal controls over grant management for federal awards. These deficiencies include the procurement of pre-2007 MY trucks that do not meet the requirements of an EPA award. The single audit also identified interest rates that were above the rate allowed in the grant agreement for the EPA SmartWay 1 grant.

-continued-

---

[7] Report on Internal Control over Financial Reporting and on Compliance and Other Matters on an Audit of Financial Statements Performed in Accordance with Government Auditing Standards, p. 3, *Cascade Sierra Solutions Reports and Schedules Required by the Single Audit Act and OMB Circular A-133, Years Ended December 31, 2010 Statements and Supplemental Information, For the Year Ended December 31, 2010, EIN 20-4463950.*

OIG Response 3 (continued).

In response to the significant deficiencies identified by this single audit, EPA designated CSS as a high-risk recipient and changed their method of payment from "advanced" to "reimbursement with documentation" in October 2011.

The EPA contracted review was a limited scope review and addressed the draws of EPA funds and initial disbursement. We reviewed the contractor's supporting workpapers but a "full listing of cash disbursements for the initial $9 million" cited by CSS was not included. The contractor's workpapers do include a spreadsheet documenting $8,297,395 of disbursements through December 31, 2009. These working papers did not show that the contractor reconciled the spreadsheet information to the accounting system. The contractor's review also confirmed that CSS had written policies and procedures covering financial management, procurement, personnel, and payroll. However, the review did not verify that the policies and procedures were being implemented. The working papers showed that the contractor performed a general review of CSS' financial management, but did not verify that the recipient was able to determine the financial position on the revolving loan fund.

Regarding CSS' comment that it provided each set of auditors with the same documentation, we acknowledge that we received the same listing or spreadsheet of expenditures the EPA contractor used to review draws under the CA. However, as discussed earlier in this OIG response, the contractor's working papers did not show that the spreadsheet information was reconciled to the accounting system. We also note that the listing of the cash disbursements for the initial $9 million included in appendix A of CSS' response to the draft report is not an accurate reproduction of the listing of expenditures provided to the EPA contractor or the OIG during the audit. The listing provided to the EPA contractor and the OIG included expenditures for only 2009. However, the listing in appendix A includes expenditures for 2009 and 2010. Regardless of the difference between the listings, we were unable to reconcile the information in the listings to the accounting system and to verify that the draws were used for expenditures meeting the terms and conditions of the CA.

1. Subsequent CSS Actions

During OIG's audit, OIG suggested an alternative financial structure for the revolving loan fund that would permit CSS to completely segregate CA funds from non-CA funds. Under OIG's suggested approach, CSS would use CA funds to finance 100 percent of certain projects, and those CA-financed projects would be used to secure other privately-financed projects. In this way, the CA would avoid commingling CA funds and non-CA funds, but would also maintain the ability to leverage CA funds.

Upon OIG's suggestion, and in consultation with the EPA Program Office, CSS implemented the OIG's model for its third SmartWay Finance (SW3) award, for which CSS had not yet disbursed funds at the time. However, such an approach was not feasible for the CA portfolio, because all CA funds had already been disbursed via blended loans and were revolving with other funds. If CSS had been aware of such an approach before it disbursed the CA funds, or been directed to implement such an approach by EPA before beginning the project, CSS would have done so. While CSS could theoretically refinance all loans in the CA portfolio and, in so doing, separate CA funds from non-CA funds, this would cost CSS at least $500,000 in pre-payment penalties to financial institutions, staff costs, and other document fees. Given CSS' non-profit status and relatively small levels of operating income, this option is prohibitively expensive, and would deter CSS from its objectives of cleaning the air, reducing fuel consumption, and saving jobs.

Although CSS understands the merits of the OIG model for the revolving loan fund that would permit segregation of CA funds, CSS believes that its commingled-funds approach to the revolving loan fund complies with the CA and other applicable authority. Thus, while CSS has implemented the OIG model for its SW3 award, CSS does not consider this to be an acknowledgement that its commingled-funds approach under the CA is inadequate or inappropriate.

OIG Response 4. We did not suggest an alternate financial structure for the revolving loan fund. Rather, we commented to CSS management during the audit that implementation of the revolving loan fund phased financial structure prescribed in the workplan for the CA would have simplified the financial management of the revolving loan program. The financial model described above in CSS' comments is similar to the financial structure for the revolving loan fund specified in the workplan. Under Phase 1, the workplan specified that CSS would use the $9 million of EPA funding along with California Proposition 1B funding to finance leases for trucks. For Phase 2, the workplan specified that CSS would use the assets acquired during Phase 1 to leverage additional financial resources such as bank loans. CSS' decision not to implement the phased financial structure specified by the workplan resulted in more complex accounting system requirements for the revolving loan program. As discussed in our report, CSS management said that the organization's accounting system was not sophisticated enough to track all sources and uses of funding as the complexity of the revolving fund increased.

We agree that CSS' use of multiple funding sources to finance leases for the revolving loan program is acceptable under the CA. However, we do not agree that CSS' financial management system for the revolving loan program meets the requirements of 40 CFR Part 30.21 and the CA as discussed in OIG Response 3.

---

ii. Lack of Documentation

Similarly, CSS disagrees with OIG's assertion that CSS documentation of CA project costs is inadequate because no notations or coding in the accounting system or on CSS' project documentation indicated that project costs were incurred under the CA. CSS intentionally purchases trucks and equipment before it knows whether the trucks and equipment will ultimately be financed with CA funds, because such an approach is most cost-effective. Rather than document the assignment of project costs to the CA on the project documentation, or in the accounting system, CSS uses spreadsheets to track project costs incurred under the CA, because this method most efficiently allows CSS to take advantage of multiple funding sources and reallocate CA funds to other projects when possible.

CSS does not immediately decide whether a project will be a permanent part of the CA portfolio because this allows the most cost-effective use of CA funds. CSS prefers to use private sector and other non-CA funds to finance truck and equipment projects whenever possible, so as to keep CA funds available for new projects. However, certain funding sources only become available for CSS projects after leases or loans are formalized with the customer. In these cases, CSS uses CA funds as initial working capital for the project, and later substitutes in non-CA funds, making the CA funds available again. This is the case with many grants, which can take several months to receive and with most of CSS' private sector partners, which will usually finance a truck or equipment project only after the lease or loan has been completely formalized and is in repayment. Thus, in order to exploit these funding opportunities and make the most effective use of taxpayer funds, CSS does not initially determine whether a truck and equipment project will be a permanent part of its CA portfolio.

An example helps to illustrate how this principle works and demonstrates why it is a necessary part of CSS' business model. In October 2009, a California Licensed Motor Carrier (fleet) began working with CSS to find a solution for its independent owner operators (IOOs) that wanted to upgrade their trucks. CSS researched available trucks and purchased a batch of trucks from USA Trucks, a truck wholesaler, with the fleet's approval. The trucks CSS purchased on behalf of the fleet were located on the East Coast and had to be shipped to the fleet's yard in California.

In the first phase of the process to put these trucks into service for the fleet and its IOOs, CSS put a deposit down on the trucks, obtained a signed memorandum of understanding from the fleet that it would purchase the trucks from CSS, set up customer leases, and then purchased the trucks and transported them to California. The memorandum of understanding included a preliminary lease calculation, which the fleet used to explain the project to the drivers and obtain commitments from the IOOs. CSS subsequently had each of the 30 IOOs planning to purchase one of the trucks sign a lease document, which is documented by the final lease calculation, before paying the vendor and transporting the trucks. Although CSS ultimately intended to obtain California Air Resources Board (CARB) funding to finance the truck retrofits, and provide private sector lenders for each of the leases associated with these trucks, CSS purchased the trucks on 10/08/09 for $624,000 using only CA funds. CSS was forced to do this because CARB funds would not become available until the trucks were licensed, registered, and physically located in California; CSS' partner banks would not finance the trucks without CSS having finalized the lease documents and titles, which also required the trucks to be in California; and USA Trucks, the vendor, would not transport the trucks to California without the vehicles first being paid for in full. Thus, CSS was forced to pay the entire cost of the trucks up front to get the process moving.

The second phase of the process involved getting the trucks, after arriving in California, inspected, repaired, and delivered to the CSS customers. CSS first titled each truck in California, which allowed CSS to submit applications for CARB diesel particulate filter retrofit grants for the trucks. For each truck, this process of titling, inspection, and repair took anywhere between three and five months to complete.

The third and final phase of the process involved arranging the ultimate financing for each of the truck leases or loans. As an initial step, CSS replaced the CA funds used to retrofit the trucks with CARB grant money when it became available. For these trucks, the CARB grant money arrived between 2-3 months after the trucks were delivered to California. CSS then submitted a project summary to its partnering financial institutions for bids. After receiving responses from its partnering financial institutions, CSS evaluated the funding proposals, including some that provided 100% funding, and others that proposed blended funding, and selected the best option for its customers. This process of arranging financing was completed in May of 2010 – nearly nine months after CSS' management and processing of these trucks began and CSS had IOOs sign leases.

This example demonstrates why it is important for CSS to avoid locking in the final funding source for a project at the beginning: because other funds may only become available well after the truck has been purchased and the loan formalized. As a result of implementing this process for all of its truck lease and equipment loans, CSS has leveraged the initial $9 million in CA funds it received to generate another $5 million in truck financing from private and state and local grant sources. That is, after initially spending $9 million of CA funds on trucks, only $3.7 million—42 percent of the original amount—are today associated with these trucks. CSS has successfully found nearly $5.3 million non CA-funds to replace the CA funds and free them up for other projects. As a result, CSS has redeployed the $5.3 million in freed-up CA funds in additional projects, putting more clean trucks on the road.

As discussed below, CSS uses spreadsheets, rather than notations on physical project documentation, or coding in its accounting system, to track CA funds through this substitution-of-funds process. CSS' spreadsheet system allows CSS to substitute private or grant funding for CA funds, and thus free up CSS monies when possible. Making physical notations on documentation is not a reliable way to track this information, and CSS' accounting system was not set up at the beginning of the project period to handle multiple funding sources for a single project. CSS thus used a spreadsheet system to track this information.

> **OIG Response 5.** CSS' comments clearly disclose that it has not established a formal revolving fund or accounts within its accounting system to track the source and application of funds. Also, the example that CSS provides does not provide a rationale for not establishing a revolving loan program that tracks the assets, liabilities, revenues, and expenses in accordance with federal requirements discussed in OIG Response 3. The purpose of the funding provided by EPA under the CA was to create a revolving loan program. The program does not require exclusion of other funding sources that contribute to the program, but CSS needs to implement internal controls that ensure funding provided by EPA is being used for eligible purposes. Programmatic Condition 2.7 requires the recipient to maintain accountability for funds and assets accrued as a result of the CA award.
>
> *-continued-*

1. Subsequent CSS Actions

CSS strongly believes that it has maintained appropriate documentation under the CA, and that its use of spreadsheets to track this information was appropriate at the start of the project period and continues to be appropriate. However, CSS does acknowledge that it has not always been easy for outside parties to review transactions involving CA funds. In recognition of this challenge, and in pursuit of greater transparency for its revolving loan fund, CSS has taken a number of steps to increase its capability to monitor its projects.

In the fourth quarter of 2010, CSS established a Compliance team which performs an independent review of each project file and coordinates advances and vendor payments with other CSS departments. Further, CSS established a project origination system and a job cost system that tracks all costs associated with individual projects, and more easily allows CSS to assign and reassign financing from multiple sources to a project. In July 2010, the job cost system was implemented for regional EPA grants. Finally, CSS is in the process of integrating the project origination system with the job cost system and its accounting system.

> **OIG Response 6.** We disagree that CSS has maintained documentation for revolving loan program project costs that meets the requirements specified by 2 CFR Part 230 and 40 CFR Part 30 as discussed in the draft report. Our review of invoices, payment documents, and accounting system entries provided by CSS to support a judgment sample of $4,336,066 expenditures identified that the documentation and entries did not include notations or coding showing that the costs were incurred under the CA. With regard to CSS' comment that the use of spreadsheets was appropriate to track information under the CA, we were not able to reconcile project information in the spreadsheets to the accounting system because most revolving fund program transactions were not segregated from other transactions in the system.
>
> We acknowledge CSS' comments identifying steps taken to increase its capability to monitor projects. However, the comments do not explain how the steps have resolved the specific accounting and documentation issues for the revolving loan program discussed in the draft report.

C. Revolving Loan Fund Requirement Not Met

The OIG Draft Report states that CSS failed to (a) establish a formal revolving fund that meets the requirements of Title 40 CFR 30.21; (b) segregate all revenues, costs, cash, and accounts receivables associated with the CA within its accounting system; (c) implement a project cost system for expenditures made under the CA; and (d) reconcile its accounts because revolving loan fund transactions were not segregated from other transactions in the system.

Each of these statements relates in some way to CSS' initial decision, made before the project period started, to use spreadsheets to track CA funds in the revolving loan fund. CSS decided that spreadsheets would be appropriate to use for tracking and reporting obligations because CSS determined, through discussion with its EPA Project Officer, that CSS only needed to report on projects undertaken with the initial $9 million in CA funds, and CSS did not need to report on projects undertaken with revolved loan funds. Because of this understanding, CSS considered a spreadsheet system to be most appropriate for CA compliance and reporting, and declined to implement a more complex tracking system.

CSS believes that its tracking of CA funds using spreadsheets constitutes compliance with the CA and EPA and OMB regulations. CSS declined to create separate lease or loan transactions for each funding source used in a project, as the Draft Report claims is required, because such a process would impose significant operational difficulties on CSS and its customers and is not feasible.[8] Such an approach would require, for each project, multiple lease or loan documents, each of which would require separate monthly payments from the borrower, and would dramatically increase loan servicing complexity and costs, internal set up, monthly processing time, and collection efforts. In addition, such an arrangement would place an untenable burden on CSS' customers, many of whom are small, independent truckers, and do not speak English as a first language.

With the deployment of the CA funds, CSS created a secondary spreadsheet database specifically for the purpose of tracking CA funds by project. This secondary database, which CSS calls its Accounts Receivable Distribution Table, allows CSS to track multiple sources of funding for a single project and to automatically designate incoming loan repayments associated with a project proportionately back to its funding sources.[9] CSS regularly reviews and reconciles this database with its lease and loan portfolios. Because of limitations in CSS' accounting system that existed at the beginning of the project period, these reviews or reconciliations are currently prepared outside of the accounting system and the net results of the activity are recorded via journal entry into the accounting system. This process of spreadsheet tracking, with periodic reviews and reconciliation with the accounting system, provides the same tracking capability as OIG's preferred approach.

---

[8] CSS understands OIG to interpret EPA and OMB regulations and the CA to require that a project with multiple funding sources (e.g., CA 5%; State Grant 50%; Financial Institution 45%) be recorded and tracked as three separate lease or loan transactions.

[9] In the deployment of the Accounts Receivable Distribution Table in March 2010, CSS incorporated categories to separately track each of its EPA SmartWay Finance Grants and other sources of funding. As stated by CSS Bylaws, any excess net assets are to be reinvested into the CSS revolving loan fund. The Accounts Receivable Distribution Table therefore incorporated a separate designation for the CSS revolving loan fund.

CSS is in the process of incorporating this secondary database into its new customer relationship management (CRM) processing system, which interfaces with the accounting system, and will have the process completed by August 2012. This integration will eliminate the need to maintain the secondary database for CA reporting, will significantly streamline CSS tracking and reporting processes, and will increase the quality and consistency of CSS reporting data.

OIG Response 7. We were not able to verify with the EPA project officer CSS' comments explaining that it considered a spreadsheet system to be most appropriate for CA compliance and reporting based on a discussion with the EPA project officer. The original project officer for the CA no longer is employed by EPA, and the current project officer was assigned to the CA in September 2010. The current project officer told us that he was not aware of any EPA guidance that would direct or suggest CSS to only report on the initial deployment of the $9 million in CA funds. This project officer also informed CSS in February 2011 to continue reporting projects in quarterly reports until the grant is closed out and the final project report is submitted to EPA.

We do not agree that CSS' use of spreadsheets constitutes compliance with 40 CFR Part 30.21 and the CA. Title 40 CFR Part 30.21(b)(2) requires recipients' financial management systems to provide records that adequately identify the source and application of funds for federally sponsored activities. Title 40 CFR Part 30.21(b)(3) further specifies that recipients' financial management systems provide accountability for funds, property and other assets. Programmatic Condition 2.7 of the CA requires the recipient to maintain effective control over and be accountable for all funds, property, and other assets accrued as a result of the CA. As discussed in the draft report, we were not able to reconcile the spreadsheets to the accounting system because most revolving loan fund transactions were not segregated from other transactions in the system.

The draft report does not state that CSS is required under federal regulations and the CA to create separate lease or loan transactions for each funding source. Rather, the report explains that we are unable to provide an opinion on the financial resources, related liabilities, revenue, expenses, and residual balances of the fund because CSS has not established and used a comprehensive set of accounts for the revolving fund. Accounting for all funding associated with the revolving loan program is consistent with the revolving loan fund model specified in the workplan for the CA. The workplan specifies that principal in the loan fund (from EPA and other contributors) will remain in the fund permanently, continuing to revolve and be used for the same purpose of clean technology leases. Therefore, all financial resources, related liabilities, revenue, expenses, and residual balances are required to be accounted for as part of the revolving loan program partly funded by the CA. CSS' comments do not explain why it is unable to establish a comprehensive set of general ledger accounts that records all revolving loan program financial transactions.

-continued-

During the course of the audit, CSS provided the OIG with a spreadsheet that includes data on lease receivables by customer as of December 31, 2010, and appears to be the "Accounts Receivable Distribution Table" described by CSS in its comments on the draft report. This spreadsheet identifies the total present value of lease receivables for all CSS customers. The spreadsheet also appears to identify projects fully or partially funded under the CA as well as projects funded under other funding sources and programs. The total present value for the projects includes all funding sources (i.e., commingled funds) used to finance the lease. Although CSS' comments disclose that the spreadsheet is periodically reconciled to the accounting system, we are unable to reconcile the lease receivable balances for projects identified as fully or partially funded under the CA to the accounting system because revolving loan fund receivables were not segregated from other receivables in the general ledger.

We acknowledge CSS' comments on the new CRM system. However, CSS has not explained how the CRM will achieve segregation of lease receivables for the revolving loan program in the accounting system.

i. A Formal Revolving Loan Fund Is Not Required Under the CA

CSS disagrees with the OIG Draft Report's statement that CSS must establish a "formal" revolving loan fund to meet the requirements of Title 40 CFR 30.21. That regulation does not prescribe any requirements for a "formal" revolving loan fund or even mention revolving loan funds in any respect. As a result, CSS does not believe that the CA, or other applicable ARRA, EPA, or OMB requirements, mandates that CSS implement a formal revolving loan fund.

At the beginning of the CA project period, CSS decided against a formal revolving loan framework for several reasons. First, a formal revolving loan fund would require CSS to formally lock in financing sources before financing a project. As described above in section III.B.ii, the ability to delay this decision provides many advantages, and allows for the most cost-effective use of taxpayer money.

Second, at the beginning of the project period, CSS did not have sufficient accounting or administrative infrastructure to implement a formal revolving loan fund. As noted above, CSS has grown rapidly in recent years and has, over the past three years, taken significant and appropriate steps to upgrade its internal control and accounting systems. Over this time period, CSS has undertaken and completed numerous compliance upgrades, including the upgrade of its accounting system; the creation of a job cost system dedicated to grants compliance (in July 2010, before the OIG audit began); and the creation and development of a customer management system that is integrated with the accounting, billing, and collection systems, incorporates grants and award requirements for both regional and national EPA awards, handles lease and loan transactions for both trucks and equipment, and allows for multiple funding sources for a single lease or loan transaction. A formal revolving loan fund disbursing blended public-private loans would require most, if not all of, these administrative functions to be available at the outset of the project. Given the resources available to CSS at the time it was awarded the CA, and given the fact that, at that time of the CA's award, most of the above accounting and administrative infrastructure was not in place, it was simply not feasible for CSS to implement a formal revolving loan fund at that point. However, the CSS system in place today provides the same result.

ii. Segregated CA Accounts Are Not Required

CSS acknowledges that it did not establish a segregated set of accounts within its accounting system for the CA, but disagrees with OIG that such a setup is required. As mentioned above, such an arrangement would significantly increase the administrative burdens associated with the revolving loan fund CSS and its customers. Moreover, in 2009 and 2010, EPA was the single largest contributor to the CSS revolving loan fund, and substantially all of CSS' operations involved the revolving loan fund. Because the CSS revolving loan fund deliberately blends resources from multiple sources, and because CSS chose to track CA funds for reporting purposes in a secondary database, CSS did not consider it necessary to segregate the cost of each financing project by funding source within its accounting system.

iii. A Project Job Cost System Is Not Required

While a Project Job Cost system aids in tracking revenue and costs by grant or contract, such a system is not required by either Title 40 CFR Part 30 or Title 2 CFR Part 230. Although CSS implemented a Project Job Cost system in July 2010, this occurred after the initial disbursement of $9 million in CA funds, which was completed in early 2010. CSS did not recreate past CA transactions associated with the revolving loan fund in its Project Job Cost system because it has not been directed to do so by EPA, and this would be a hugely burdensome undertaking. To fully switch to the Project Job Cost system for the entire CA project period, CSS would have to reclassify each transaction associated with the revolving loan fund that has taken place since the beginning of the CA project period, which started on June 1, 2009. The revolved loan fund now involves 8,500 transactions per month, so reclassifying 30 months of past transactions would be a truly massive undertaking. However, CSS intends to set up all future grants and contracts within its Project Job Cost system.

OIG Response 8. We disagree with CSS' position that the CA or federal regulations do not require a formal revolving fund. The CA award provided Recovery Act funding to CSS for the creation of a national revolving loan program and specified that the recipient comply with 40 CFR Part 30. The workplan for the CA specified that CSS will implement a revolving loan fund using multiple funding sources. The workplan further specified that principal in the loan fund (from EPA and other contributors) will remain in the fund permanently, continuing to revolve, and be used for the same purpose of clean technology leases. The workplan also stated that CSS will not use any EPA funding to pay program operating costs but would use interest earned from the program.

-continued-

OIG Response 8 (continued).

Title 40 CFR Part 30 and the CA include provisions to ensure complete accounting for all the funds, property, and assets accrued as a result of the CA. Title 40 CFR Part 30.21(b)(2) clearly specifies that financial management systems should provide records that contain information pertaining to "assets, outlays, income and interest." Title 40 CFR Part 30.21(b)(3) requires that the financial management system provide "effective control over and accountability for all funds, property and other assets." Title 40 CFR Part 30.21(b)(3) also states that "recipients shall adequately safeguard all such assets and assure they are used solely for authorized purposes." Programmatic Condition 2.5.A of the CA is consistent with 40 CFR Part 30 and requires that the recipient maintain records to track Recovery Act funds separately from other grant programs. Programmatic Condition 2.7 of the CA requires the recipient to be accountable for funds, property, and other assets accrued as a result of the CA. Further, Programmatic Condition 20 requires work under the agreement to be completed in accordance with the approved workplan.

We disagree that CSS' system in place today provides the same result as a formal revolving fund established and managed through an accounting system. The complexity of the revolving loan program transactions described in CSS' comments to the draft report highlights the need to establish a formal revolving fund that meets the financial management requirements of federal regulations and the CA. CSS' revolving loan program includes funding from multiple sources, lease receivables, loan payables, program income, and expenses. Therefore, a dedicated set of general ledger accounts is necessary to define the scope of the revolving loan fund and account for all funds and assets accrued as a result of the CA award. Without records that reconcile to the accounting system, we are unable to determine whether funds were used under the revolving loan program in accordance with the terms and conditions of the CA. We found no evidence during the examination that CSS' accounting system lacked the capacity to establish a formal revolving loan fund through a dedicated set of general ledger accounts at the time of the CA award.

We disagree that a project cost system is not required by either 40 CFR Part 30 or 2 CFR Part 230. The CA award provided CSS with $9 million in Recovery Act funds specifically to create a revolving loan program for heavy-duty trucks to save fuel and reduce emissions. Title 40 CFR Part 30.21(b)(2) specifies that a recipient's financial management systems shall provide records that adequately identify the source and application of funds for federally sponsored activities. In addition, 2 CFR Part 230, Appendix A, A.2(a) and (g), require costs to be allocable and adequately documented to be considered allowable under an award. A project cost system accounts for costs by a specific project or program rather than by department or the overall organization. Therefore, a project cost system is required by these regulations to show that the expenditures for the revolving loan program are specifically allocable to and allowable under the CA.

-continued-

With regard to CSS' comments that a project job cost system was implemented in 2010, we found that CSS' general ledger covering 2010 financial transactions included only one revenue account that contained $78,000 of the $9 million award and six salary and salary-related accounts that totaled $277,431 in expenses for the revolving loan fund program. We found no general ledger accounts for trucks and other equipment expenditures under the revolving loan program partly funded by the $9 million CA award. Therefore, we agree that fully accounting for the $9 million award would be a difficult undertaking for CSS. However, CSS is required under 40 CFR Part 30 to fully account for the Recovery Act funding. CSS' comment that it intends to set up all future grants and contracts within its project cost system will not provide acceptable accountability for the $9 million award of Recovery Act funds.

D. Project Costs Not Fully Supported

The OIG Draft Report states that CSS was unable to provide complete support for revolving loan program projects and associated lessee payments because the projects and payments were either understated or overstated. The OIG Draft Report also states that CSS was unable to accurately identify income or losses from leases or measure whether leases and the revolving fund program were economically sound because CSS failed to meet applicable financial management requirements.

Again, CSS disagrees with OIG's assertions. CSS told OIG during the audit, and OIG's audit bore out, that the discrepancy OIG identified between project receipts and costs for the audited costs is due to CSS' deliberate approach of estimating, rather than precisely tracking, the costs associated with the repair of trucks. Trying to itemize this level of detail would be counterproductive from a cost perspective, and, for three reasons, CSS does not believe such an approach is feasible.

First, practical considerations require an estimated approach. CSS' business model requires borrowers to sign fixed price contracts before CSS purchases the trucks to ensure the borrower is committed to the project. However, the repair costs associated with a particular truck can vary and are not known until after CSS takes delivery of the truck, which occurs only after the borrower has signed a contract with CSS.

Second, efficiency considerations make CSS' estimated approach highly preferential. CSS makes necessary repairs to the trucks that it finances using both new and used parts. If CSS is required to align precisely its costs and receipts for each repair project it undertakes, this would require a comprehensive inventory system that tracks individual repair parts. Merely tracking general prices of commonly used parts would not be sufficient, because the prices at which CSS purchases various parts can vary from day to day and from order to order. For example, CSS normally purchases tires in bulk in order to receive the lowest prices possible. However, the price of a single tire may vary based on the model of tire; its condition; and the batch in which CSS buys the tire. While CSS could theoretically create an inventory system to calculate and record the individual prices of individual parts, it would be hugely burdensome. Moreover, such a system would still not adequately track certain repair costs including oil changes, lube jobs, and repainting (when necessary), which do not always involve measurable or discrete amounts of inventory.

Third, and most importantly, the benefits associated with implementing such a tracking system are very small, and are significantly outweighed by the corresponding administrative costs. CSS' experience indicates that a $500 repair charge accurately reflects the average cost associated with the repair of the used trucks it purchases. This charge comprises, on average, less than three percent of the cost of each truck. The OIG reviewed financing projects that totaled $229,350 and reported a net discrepancy of $909, which represents 0.4 percent of the total cost of those projects. CSS does not believe such a small differential represents a material discrepancy. Thus, CSS believes the benefit from implementing such a system would be minimal.

However, the costs associated with implementing such an inventory tracking system in CSS' truck department would be highly burdensome. Such a system would require CSS to (a) require its vendors to provide a unit-by-unit breakdown of the cost associated with the parts it purchases; (b) physically label each part that it purchases with an identifier; (c) input that identifier into the CSS project database and associate it with the purchase receipt; and (d) update the project database each time a part is used on a particular truck. Given that CSS may install several parts on a truck while repairing it, requiring such particularized information would greatly multiply the administrative burden placed on CSS accounting staff and its truck department, with little appreciable benefit.

Further, even if CSS were able to implement such an inventory system, the cost associated with truck repair would go up significantly. Under such a system, CSS would likely cease to buy parts in bulk in advance, and instead only buy repair parts upon the knowledge that such parts are needed for particular repairs. This means CSS would buy them in smaller quantities and at higher prices. Thus, implementing an inventory part tracking system would likely lead to more expensive parts, and CA funds would not be used as cost effectively as they are currently—a counter-productive result.

CSS strongly believes that its repair cost system complies with the requirements set out in EPA regulations, and the CA, and that CSS adequately identifies the source and application of the CA funds used for repairs of trucks. Given that a comprehensive inventory system is unlikely to be able to adequately track all pieces of inventory, would place a significant burden on CSS' truck department, and would not adequately document all inventory that CSS uses to repair its trucks, CSS believes that its approach is the most prudent use of CA funds and constitutes compliance with the CA and EPA and OMB regulations.

OIG Response 9. Our position remains unchanged. CSS' comments disclose that project costs include estimated repair costs rather than actual costs. CSS' comments further disclose that parts purchased in bulk are not included in an inventory tracking system and allocated to projects based on actual costs. As discussed in the draft report, 2 CFR Part 230, Appendix A, A.2 (a) and (g), require costs to be allocable and adequately documented to be considered allowable under an award. In addition, 40 CFR Part 30.21(b)(2) requires recipients' financial management systems to include records that identify adequately the source and application of funds for federally sponsored activities. This regulation further states that these records should include information pertaining to assets, outlays, income, and interest. CSS was unable to support that all reported projects costs are allowable under 2 CFR Part 230 and 40 CFR Part 30.

In the absence of a fully implemented project cost system, we were unable to determine whether the cost records that CSS provided were complete or that the costs were allocable to the CA. We were also unable to determine whether CSS' cost estimates were accurate or project costs were materially over- or under-stated. CSS was unable to accurately identify income or losses from leases or measure whether leases and the revolving fund program were economically sound because it did not meet the financial management requirements of 40 CFR Part 30.

E. Progress Reporting Not Accurate

The OIG Draft Report states that CSS' progress report for the quarter ending December 2010 did not accurately identify expenditures by funding source, the number of projects, and the total costs of projects in the revolving fund program. OIG asserts that this led to an overstatement of the number of projects financed by CA funds and an understatement of the total project costs and funding from other sources.

CSS agrees with OIG that the CSS progress report for the quarter ending in December 2010 did contain certain errors that led to inaccurately reported results. Certain figures contained errors due to oversight or improper calculation by CSS. For instance, the amended report submitted by CSS removed 39 projects, because CSS discovered during an internal audit that those projects took place outside of the CA project period. CSS also amended the report to include previously excluded total down payments and state and local grants, and the current outstanding balance of each lease or loan funded by the CA. This had the effect of increasing total project costs, down payments, and state funded expenditures. The amended report also reflects reimbursements from financial institutions for vehicles initially funded by the CA, which decreased the cumulative CA expenditures and increased financial institution expenditures by approximately $5.4 million.

However, CSS believes that most of the reporting discrepancies that OIG identified in the report are not due to error, but instead due a misunderstanding over the scope of the progress reports in question. CSS, in submitting the December 2010 and other progress reports, followed instructions it received from its EPA Project Officer to report only upon projects funded by the initial deployment of the $9 million in CA funds, and to exclude any projects funded with revolved funds. Thus, neither the original nor the amended progress report included approximately $3.8 million of emission control devices funded solely through CA revolved funds.

CSS believes that, even if EPA determines that its Project Officer's guidance was erroneous, discrepancies arising due to CSS' reliance on that guidance should not be considered erroneous. CSS' EPA Project Officer serves as its primary contact for the EPA Program Office. Given the innovative nature of the CSS revolving loan fund, CSS relied upon its Project Officer, as its principal point of contact with EPA, to provide accurate guidance on the nature of its CA obligations. Given that CSS complied with, and relied upon in good faith, its Project Officer's instructions, if EPA does determine, two years after the fact, that the Project Officer's instructions were given in error, CSS should not be held responsible for any errors that directly resulted from CSS' compliance with the erroneous instructions.

OIG Response 10. Our position remains unchanged. CSS agrees that the progress report for the quarter ending December 2010 is inaccurate and that certain figures in the report contained errors due to oversight or improper calculation. CSS' comments also acknowledge that the amended quarterly report ending December 2010 is inaccurate and excludes approximately $3.8 million of emission equipment apparently funded under the CA. As discussed in the draft report, Programmatic Condition 5 of the CA requires CSS to provide EPA with quarterly reports that address progress toward achieving the workplan goals. The condition specifies that the reports include summary information on planned activities, implementation of diesel emission reduction strategies, expenditures, and issuance of loans, leases, or bonds. Without accurate quarterly reporting by CSS, EPA is unable to measure the recipient's progress toward achieving the goals of the CA.

With regard to CSS' comment that it believes most of the reporting discrepancies identified in the draft report were caused from following guidance provided by the EPA project officer, we were unable to confirm the comment with EPA. The current project officer was assigned to the CA during September 2010 and told us that he was not aware of any EPA guidance that would direct or suggest CSS to only report on the initial deployment of the $9 million in CA funds. This project officer also informed CSS in February 2011 to continue reporting projects in quarterly reports until the grant is closed out and the final project report is submitted to EPA.

CSS' comments indicate that there appears to be a misunderstanding with EPA on the quarterly reporting requirement specified by the CA. Therefore, we have added a recommendation that EPA provide clarifying guidance to CSS on financial and other project information required to be included in quarterly progress reports and request the recipient to submit corrected progress reports as appropriate for prior quarters of the project period in the final report.

i. Subsequent CSS Actions

As the OIG Draft Report indicated, CSS submitted a new progress report for the quarter ending in December 2010 to correct certain errors due to oversight or improper calculation. However, CSS has not updated its quarterly progress reports to incorporate the use of revolved funds because it has not received instructions to do so, and such an undertaking would require a review of all transactions associated with the CA funds that have revolved, which would entail significant effort and expenditure of administrative resources. However, CSS stands ready to do so if EPA deems such action necessary.

> **OIG Response 11.** As discussed in the report, 40 CFR Part 30.21(b)(2) requires the recipient's financial management systems to include records that adequately identify the source and application of funds for federally sponsored activities. CSS' acknowledgment that significant effort and expenditure of administrative resources would be required to report on all transactions associated with the CA funds indicates that the organization is unable to readily account for all sources and application of funds of the revolving loan fund partly funded by the CA. Therefore, CSS' response further supports our position that the recipient's financial management system does not meet federal requirements under the CA and has not accurately reported on work progress toward meeting workplan goals in quarterly progress reports. We have added a recommendation that EPA require the recipient to submit corrected progress reports based on CSS' comments.

F. OIG Recommendations

i. Questioned Costs

OIG has recommended that EPA disallow and recover $9 million in questioned costs claimed under the CA, unless CSS provides documentation that meets appropriate federal financial management requirements and shows that some or all of the questioned costs are allocable and allowable to the CA. CSS believes that it has complied with all federal financial management requirements and shown all costs to be allocable and allowable under the CA. CSS has provided documentation of its expenditure of funds under the CA in Appendix A.

> **OIG Response 12.** Our position remains unchanged. As discussed in the draft report, CSS was unable to support that all funds drawn under the CA were used for expenditures that are allowable under and allocable to the CA during our examination. We were also unable to provide an opinion on the financial resources, related liabilities, revenue, expenses, and residual balances of the revolving fund. The expenditure documentation provided by CSS in appendix A of the response to the draft report does not provide any new information to support that the $9 million award has been used for expenditures that are allowable under and allocable to the CA or that any revolved funds are available for other revolving loan program projects.

ii. Suspension and Debarment

CSS strongly disagrees with OIG's recommendation that EPA consider the suspension and debarment of CSS. Neither is an appropriate course of action, and OIG has provided no evidence to suggest that such an inquiry is warranted. As a non-profit organization, CSS has been funded principally by EPA and DOE, which together have entrusted CSS with $41 million in funds over the past five years. Suspension or debarment would be severely injurious to CSS' mission, and would severely restrict its ability to lend. For this reason, CSS takes this recommendation very seriously and strongly disagrees with it.

Debarment is not an appropriate remedy because the OIG Draft Report has not claimed, or produced any evidence suggesting, that the criteria for debarment under Title 2 CFR 180.800 might be met. No CSS personnel have been convicted of any crime regarding, and neither CSS nor any of its personnel have been found civilly liable for any act regarding, the administration of any of CSS' programs or the CA. OIG has not suggested that CSS has willfully violated the terms of the CA, or EPA or OMB regulations. Far from it, CSS has consistently endeavored in good faith to comply with all requests and guidance made by the EPA Program Office concerning the CA. CSS has no history of failure to perform under any of its agreements with EPA or DOE, and has fully complied with all of its other agreements with EPA and DOE. The provisions of § 180.800(c) are not applicable, and CSS' responsibility has not been called into question, as § 180.800(d) requires. Because the OIG Draft Report outlines no facts that in any way implicate any of the regulatory criteria for debarment, EPA should not consider debarment of CSS.

Further, suspension is not warranted, because OIG has not claimed, or offered any evidence to suggest, that the criteria for suspension outlined in Title 2 CFR 180.700 might be met. No member of CSS personnel has been indicted for any criminal offense, and no evidence exists that would lead to suspicion of any criminal offense or civil liability as required by Title 2 CFR 180.700 (a). OIG has offered no evidence to suspect any other cause for debarment, including willful violations of the CA terms or EPA or OMB regulations; a history of failure of CSS to perform under other agreements; any cause listed in Title 2 CFR 180.800(c); or doubt about CSS' present responsibility. Finally, no immediate action is necessary to protect the public interest. Indeed, if EPA undertakes suspension or debarment of CSS, such action would have the perverse effect of significantly *harming* the public interest, because such action would forgo the emissions reductions, public health benefits, and fuel savings associated with the CSS program, and would deny thousands of future CSS customers access to funding for their small businesses. Thus, because the regulatory criteria for suspension are not met, and the public interest would be harmed, rather than protected, by suspending CSS, EPA should not consider suspension of CSS.

Other considerations further buttress the conclusion that EPA should not consider the suspension or debarment of EPA. CSS' auditor, Isler CPA, has prepared a letter, attached as Appendix B to this report, which notes that it is not aware of any evidence that would support consideration of suspension or debarment of CSS. Moreover, suspension or debarment are actions of last resort, and are premature, because CSS stands ready to work with EPA and OIG to resolve the audit to the satisfaction of all parties. Because of CSS' good faith efforts to comply with EPA directives, and because of the novel nature of CSS' public-private revolving loan fund,

EPA should first consider whether specific guidance would remedy any deficiencies or shortcomings it may find and give CSS a chance to comply with such guidance. Thus, because OIG has not shown or suggested that the criteria set out in EPA's regulations for suspension and debarment might be met, and because CSS is willing to work diligently in implementing the guidance of EPA as the revolving loan fund continues to evolve, CSS respectfully requests that EPA not consider suspension and debarment.

OIG Response 13. Our position remains unchanged. Title 2 CFR Part 180.800(b) specifies that an Agency may pursue a suspension and debarment action for violations of the terms of a public agreement or transaction so serious as to affect the integrity of an agency program. As discussed in the draft report, the $9 million awarded to CSS represents 30 percent of the Recovery Act awards under the SmartWay Clean Diesel Finance Program. Therefore, CSS' financial management deficiencies discussed in the draft report pose a serious threat to the integrity of the Recovery Act-funded portion of EPA's Clean Diesel Finance Program.

We also disagree with CSS' position that the recipient has no performance or compliance deficiencies under any of its agreements with EPA. During October 2011, EPA's Office of Grants and Debarment designated CSS as a "high-risk" recipient as a result of material noncompliance with the terms and conditions of several federal awards discussed in its single audit report for the year ended December 31, 2010. Because of the designation, the Office of Grants and Debarment changed CSS' method of payment under EPA awards from "advance" to "reimbursement with documentation" for all active awards. A history of failure to perform or unsatisfactory performance under one or more public agreements is another of the criteria for suspension and debarment under 2 CFR Part 180. CSS financial management issues under the CA and material noncompliance issues under other federal awards identified in the single audit report establish a history of failure to perform under federal agreements.

We acknowledge the letter from CSS' Certified Public Accountant commenting that they did not find any material noncompliance with federal regulations or requirements of the award during the single audit. However, the single audit report covering the year ended December 31, 2010, does not discuss the specific requirements of the CA, present any financial details of the revolving loan program partly funded by the EPA award, or the financial position of the revolving loan fund.

CSS' comments to the draft report indicate that it does not fully understand the financial management requirements specified by 40 CFR Part 30, 2 CFR Part 230, and the CA. These regulations and the terms and conditions of the award include provisions that require CSS' financial management system to provide accountability for funds and other assets. Without segregated accounts for all funds and assets, we are unable to determine whether funds, including revolved funds, are being used in accordance with the terms and conditions of the CA. We also cannot determine whether CSS can meet operating expenses of the program with program income or if expenses are in fact eroding the capital provided by EPA and other sources.

---

iii. Establishment of Internal Controls

OIG also recommends that CSS establish controls that ensure the use of CA funding complies with Title 40 CFR 30.21. Such controls should ensure (a) accurate, current, and complete disclosure of the financial results of the revolving loan program funded under the CA; (b) records that identify adequately the source and application of CA funds; and (c) effective control over and accountability for all funds, property, and other assets of the EPA-funded revolving loan program.

The steps CSS has taken prior to, and in response to, the concerns laid out in the OIG Draft Report should eliminate any doubt that CSS has sufficient controls in place to respond these concerns. CSS has implemented a job cost system that meets OIG and EPA's concerns, interfaces with CSS' accounting system, and adequately tracks projects with funding from multiple sources. Further, based on OIG's suggestion, CSS has implemented a new financial structure that avoids the commingling of CA and non-CA funds in its SW3 award. Finally, CSS has created a 3-member compliance department that did not exist at the beginning of the CA project period and that is solely dedicated to ensuring CSS meets its reporting obligations under the CA, other EPA and DOE awards, and all relevant federal statutes, regulations, and guidance.

CSS believes that it has always complied with its obligations to report and track CA funds, but emphasizes that its capacity to administer a complex financial structure, such as its revolving loan fund, has grown immensely over the past three years. Should EPA require further steps to ensure that CSS' internal controls are sufficient, CSS stands ready to discuss how any such controls can be implemented in a reasonable manner.

OIG Response 14. Our position remains unchanged. With regard to CSS' comment that it has implemented a job cost system, our examination of the recipient's accounting system and supporting documentation disclosed that a job (or project) cost system has not been fully implemented for the revolving fund. As discussed in the draft report, CSS' general ledger included only one revenue account that contained $78,000 of the $9 million award and six salary and salary-related accounts that totaled $277,431 in expenses for the revolving loan fund program. We found no general ledger accounts for truck and other equipment expenditures for the revolving loan program even though CSS has claimed that the majority of the $9 million award has been deployed for eligible projects. Further, our review of supporting records for a judgmental sample of $4,336,066 in expenditures CSS associated with the $9 million in cash draws under the CA showed no project coding. As a result, we were unable to verify that the expenditures were allocable to and allowable under the CA. We were also unable to provide an opinion on the assets, liabilities, revenues, and expenses for the revolving loan program because of the lack of a comprehensive set of accounts for the revolving loan program. CSS has not explained changes to its accounting system that ensure the use of funding provided under the CA complies with 40 CFR Part 30.21. CSS will need to explain these changes in response to the final report.

-continued-

OIG Response 14 (continued).

We acknowledge CSS' comment that a new financial structure has been implemented for its EPA SmartWay 3 award. However, CSS has not explained how the new financial structure for the SmartWay 3 award resolves the financial management issues and establishes internal controls that ensure the use of funding provided under the CA is in compliance with 40 CFR Part 30.21. CSS will need to explain the internal controls in its response to the final report.

Although CSS commented that a three-member compliance department has been created to ensure compliance with federal regulations and award requirements, the recipient has not explained the internal controls implemented by this department to achieve compliance. CSS will need to explain these internal controls in its response to the final report.

We do not agree that CSS has always complied with its obligations to report and track CA funds. As discussed in the draft report, we were unable to verify that CSS used the $9 million of EPA funding for expenditures that are allocable to and allowable under the CA. We are also unable to provide an opinion on the financial resources, related liabilities, revenue, expenses, and residual balances of the revolving fund because of material noncompliance and internal control weaknesses with financial management.

iv. Special Conditions on Future EPA Awards

OIG has also recommended that EPA awards to CSS include special conditions requiring payment on a reimbursement basis, subject to approval by the EPA Project Officer, until EPA agrees that CSS has met all applicable federal financial management requirements. CSS concurs with this approach, with the following caveat.

CSS respectfully urges EPA to apply such special conditions only to CSS' EPA SmartWay Finance awards and to exempt its regional awards from such treatment. These regional awards are straightforward to administer and EPA has never had questions concerning their implementation. However, they are very capital-intensive. Because CSS' size is small when compared to the amount of money that it distributes through these grants, CSS does not have the ability to spend money extensively out of pocket and be reimbursed later. Because of CSS' lack of working capital, reimbursement status on these grants works a serious financial hardship on CSS. That was recently illustrated in vivid detail when an unexpected month-long delay in reimbursement by EPA nearly resulted in legal action against CSS by one of its vendors that had not been paid as a result of the delay. Given that the transactions occurring under these grants are straightforward and do not involve the revolving loan fund in any way, EPA should not place any special conditions on CSS' regional grants.

> **OIG Response 15.** Our position on the recommendation remains unchanged. During October 2011, EPA's Office of Grants and Debarment designated CSS as a "high-risk" recipient as a result of material noncompliance with the terms and conditions of several federal (including EPA) awards discussed in its single audit report for the year ended December 31, 2010. Because of the designation, the Office of Grants and Debarment changed CSS' method of payment under EPA awards from "Advance" to "Reimbursement with Documentation" for all active awards. Therefore, EPA has already established the recommended special conditions for all active awards.
>
> CSS' response to the draft report further supports the necessity for full implementation of the recommendation. CSS' response discloses that the recipient has not resolved the financial management issues identified in the report and does not fully understand the financial management requirements specified by federal regulations and the CA. EPA should establish the special conditions for future awards until CSS is able to fully demonstrate compliance with federal financial management requirements.

IV.   Comments on Chapter 4 – Procurement Requirements

A. Truck Procurements Did Not Follow Competitive Process

The OIG Draft Report states that CSS' truck procurements did not meet the requirements of Title 40 CFR Part 30, or CSS' own procurement policy, because CSS procured trucks without following a formal and documented competitive process. While CSS acknowledges that it did not comply with applicable procurement requirements for its truck purchases, this is only because CSS did not think those procurement requirements were applicable. CSS strongly believes that its purchasing decisions have always been in the best interests of its consumers, and that its ability to purchase trucks from wholesalers and fleets at below market value has consistently resulted in excellent value for its customers. Thus, while CSS disagrees with OIG's application of the procurement requirements to its truck purchases, CSS is confident that it can provide a sound and reasonable basis for each of the purchasing decisions questioned in the OIG Draft Report.

CSS has always understood its obligations to follow EPA, and its own, procurement policy when appropriate. This is evidenced by a competitive bid process that CSS undertook in 2008 for new model year 2009 diesel trucks from truck manufacturers. However, after evaluating the bids it received, CSS realized that new trucks were not feasible for most of its target audience, and shifted its focus to used trucks, which are a more cost-effective and realistic option for its customers.

CSS does not believe that the procurement regulations should apply to its used truck purchases because, in acquiring the trucks, CSS acts as an agent of its customers. Because there is a lack of uniformity in the trucks available on the used heavy-duty diesel truck market, and because CSS borrowers have different budgets and different needs for their trucks, CSS borrowers need to be able to select their own used trucks. They are the only ones who can realistically make a decision as to whether a particular used truck at a particular price is acceptable. Because CSS customers make the final decision on whether to accept a truck, CSS views itself as a middleman buying wholesale trucks on behalf of retail borrowers, and views the procurement requirements as inapplicable in such a context.

CSS confirmed that its interpretation of the procurement rules in this respect was acceptable by consulting with its EPA Project Officer, who agreed with CSS that its approach to purchasing vehicles did not constitute procurement: "While CSS lists eligible vehicles available from multiple dealers, CSS isn't directly selecting the vehicles because it is decided by the driver…. [t]his approach sounded reasonable in trying to ensure open competition for selection the most appropriate vehicles."[10]

However, CSS now understands OIG and the EPA Program Office to consider this CSS wholesaling activity to be a procurement activity subject to the requirements of Title 40 CFR 30.45. CSS does not contest this interpretation.

As a result of this change in procurement policy, CSS has implemented a price analysis procedure that it believes complies with Title 40 CFR 30.45. Under this procedure, whenever CSS purchases a truck or fleet of trucks, it documents that the purchase price is competitive with the prices of other comparable used trucks, as indicated by North American Dealer Association (NADA) valuations and industry publications, such as Truck Paper.

CSS has also applied this procedure retroactively to confirm that each of its truck purchases conducted under the CA resulted in prices lower than those that could have been obtained using federal procurement procedures. The results of this comparison are available in Appendix C.

OIG Response 16. We acknowledge CSS' statement that it now understands that truck procurements under the CA are subject to 40 CFR Part 30.45. However, we disagree the EPA project officer for the CA agreed that CSS' approach to purchasing vehicles did not constitute procurement. CSS' comment is based on an April 15, 2010, e-mail from the EPA project officer that discloses she understands that the selection of vehicles for purchase is made by the drivers rather than CSS. The e-mail does not instruct CSS to ignore the cost or price analysis, competition, and other documentation requirements specified by 40 CFR Part 30 as discussed in the draft report. As discussed in the report, CSS is also obligated to meet both the competition and other documentation requirements specified by 40 CFR Part 30.46 for purchases exceeding $100,000.

CSS' recently implemented price analysis procedure should meet the price analysis requirements of 40 CFR Part 30.45 if completed analyses show vehicle purchase prices are fair and reasonable and are fully documented. However, the results of CSS' retroactive application of the procedure for truck purchases included in appendix C of its response does

-continued-

---

[10] Email from Annie Kee to Sharon Banks, dated April 15, 2010, Appendix C, page C-2.

OIG Response 16 (continued).

not resolve the truck procurement issues discussed in the draft report. CSS provided in appendix C a document showing a retroactive comparison of purchase prices with National Automobile Dealers Association (NADA) retail values for a sample of 425 trucks placed in service during 2010. The comparison identifies that all 425 trucks in the sample were purchased at a price below the retail NADA value. Although CSS disclosed that the sample was representative of trucks placed in service in 2010, we were unable to determine whether the sample provided sufficient coverage of vehicle procurements allocable to the CA because the methodology was not included in appendix C. We were also unable to verify the accuracy of CSS' price analysis for two primary reasons. First, the comparison data did not include the mileage for 178 of the trucks even though mileage is one of the factors used in determining the NADA value of a vehicle. Second, documentation supporting truck model, purchase price, and other data presented in the comparison document was not included in appendix C.

B. Documented Cost or Price Analysis for Emission Control Equipment Procurements

Like its policy on truck purchases, CSS did not, until recently, consider EPA and CSS' own procurement requirements to apply to emission control equipment purchases made on behalf of CSS borrowers. This was the case for two reasons. First, as with its truck purchases, CSS does not consider itself to be the procurer of emission control equipment, but rather an agent acting on behalf of its borrowers. Second, CSS, in financing emission control equipment, never takes ownership or possession of the emission control equipment. CSS merely acts as a broker for such equipment, and allows the customer to select the exhaust retrofit that is installed by an authorized dealer.

However, CSS now understands OIG and the EPA Program Office to consider CSS financing of emission control equipment to constitute a procurement activity for purposes of EPA procurement requirements and, as such, must be justified by a cost or price analysis. CSS does not contest this interpretation.

As it has done with its truck purchases, CSS has instituted a procedure for price analysis of emission control equipment. In many cases, only one option is available to a customer because CARB has only one verified technology for the specific engine type. In such cases, CSS documents that this is the case. Further, CSS periodically issues requests for proposals, using industry publications and/or valuation tools, to ensure that it accurately provides current prices to customers making decisions about which emission control equipment to buy through CSS.

OIG Response 17. We acknowledge CSS' statement that it now understands that expenditures for emission control equipment under the CA are required by 40 CFR Part 30.45 to be supported by a cost or price analysis. We also acknowledge CSS' statement that it has instituted a procedure for price analysis of emission control equipment. However, CSS' comments do not disclose and include documentation supporting that the recipient has completed cost or price analyses for the $4,987,923 in reported costs incurred for truck emission control equipment discussed in the draft report. Therefore, CSS' comments have not resolved the cost or price analysis issue for these equipment procurements.

C. Retrofit of 227 Pre-2007 Model Year Trucks

The OIG Draft Report states that the costs associated with 227 pre-MY 2007 trucks are not allowable because the trucks have not yet been retrofitted with emission control technologies. Although these trucks were not retrofitted immediately after their purchase due to an unforeseen but significant delay, they are being retrofitted now and will be completed by June 17, 2012.

CSS did not retrofit the trucks immediately upon purchasing them because it anticipated receiving CARB grant funds for the trucks shortly after they were purchased that would enable CSS to install much more effective retrofits on the trucks. CSS purchased the trucks on behalf of California buyers and decided not to install diesel oxidation catalyst (DOC) retrofits, which were the most economical retrofits allowable under the CA, because the DOCs would only reduce 20% of particulate matter emissions, and would only be valid in California through the end of 2012. Instead, CSS planned to utilize CARB grants to install diesel particulate filters (DPFs), which reduce 85% of particulate matter emissions, and are permitted in California after 2012. CSS viewed the decision to forgo DOC retrofits and wait for DPFs instead as a reasonable one, because it would achieve greater emissions reductions and eliminate the need for truckers to upgrade their trucks again after 2013 to maintain compliance with the new, tougher California emissions standards.

CSS did not make the decision to pursue DPFs imprudently. In the year prior to purchasing these trucks, CSS had successfully applied for, and secured, approximately 300 CARB grants for DPFs, and CSS had no reason to think that it would not be successful in securing CARB grants for the 227 trucks. Further, CSS confirmed this course of action in writing with its EPA Project Officer before deciding against the DOC retrofits.[11]

In April 2011, after a one-year delay, CSS was informed by CARB that the 2006 model year truck projects would not qualify for the CARB retrofit grant due to a rule change after the purchase of the trucks. Since then, CSS has been researching other options to implement the proposed strategy. After finding no other solutions, CSS is now installing the DOCs.

CSS completed a bid process for the equipment and installation process of the DOCs and ordered the retrofits in November 2011. Although CSS encountered a slight delay in installation because the State of California had not approved the technology as CARB verified, CSS' DOC vendor, Johnson Matthey, received an "After Market Parts Exemption" to allow the installation of these retrofits on February 8, 2012. CSS plans to follow the schedule it set out in a letter dated October 31, 2011 to the EPA Program Office, and finish the retrofits of the 227 pre-2007 MY trucks by June 17, 2012.

---

[11] Email from Annie Kee to Sharon Banks, dated April 15, 2010, Appendix C, page C-2.

OIG Response 18. Our position remains unchanged. Programmatic Condition 3.1.G of the CA specifies that CSS may use the funding under the award to purchase or lease pre-2007 MY on-highway vehicles, used engines, and used pieces of equipment as long as verified emission control technologies have been installed. CSS' comments disclosed that the emission control equipment retrofits for the pre-2007 MY trucks had not been completed as of February 21, 2012, the date of its response to the draft report.

We acknowledge CSS' comment that its decision to pursue diesel particulate filters rather than diesel oxidation catalyst retrofits was confirmed in writing with the EPA project officer. This confirmation was in the form of an April 15, 2010, e-mail to CSS from the EPA project officer disclosing that she was aware of the recipient's plan to install the diesel particulate filters. The e-mail also disclosed that the project officer was aware that this process may take a "little bit of time." As of February 2012, we note the emission control equipment retrofits for the pre-2007 MY trucks had not been completed as required by the CA even though almost two years had elapsed since the project officer sent the April 2010 email to CSS.

CSS' comments also disclose that the recipient's current plan to install diesel oxidation catalyst retrofits rather than diesel particulate filters by June 2012 does not satisfactorily resolve the CA compliance issue with the pre-2007 MY trucks. CSS' comments disclose that the diesel oxidation catalyst retrofits are only valid as emission control equipment through 2012, and equipment meeting more stringent emissions standards will be required for the trucks in 2013. Therefore, the retrofitted trucks will not achieve emissions standards over the long-term. Consequently, the expenditures for the pre-2007 MY trucks do not represent effective and efficient use of Recovery Act funds and are not reasonable costs under the CA.

D. CSS Response to OIG Recommendations

i. Compliance with Title 40 CFR Part 30.45 and 30.46

The OIG Draft Report recommends that CSS be required to comply, at a minimum, with EPA procurement requirements for past and future procurements under the CA by (a) maintaining in the procurement records the minimum documentation required by Title 40 CFR 30.46 for procurements exceeding $100,000, and (b) conducting and maintaining in the procurement records a cost or price analysis for every procurement action.

In response to OIG and EPA direction, CSS has retroactively complied with EPA's procurement requirements for its past procurements. It now maintains the minimum documentation required for each procurement CSS has conducted over $100,000 and a cost or price analysis for every procurement action it has conducted. For future procurements, CSS will maintain the minimum required documentation for procurements over $100,000 and will conduct a cost or price analysis for every procurement action it undertakes.

> **OIG Response 19.** CSS did not specifically state whether it agreed with the recommendation. However, CSS' comments indicate concurrence with the recommended corrective action. With regard to CSS' comment that it retroactively complied with EPA's procurement requirements for past procurements, we were unable to verify whether the corrective actions satisfactorily resolve the documentation and analyses issues because sufficient information and supporting documentation was not included in the response to the draft report as discussed in **OIG Responses 16 and 17**.

ii. Disallowance of Pre-2007 MY Trucks as Project Costs

The OIG Draft Report also recommends that EPA disallow the pre-2007 MY trucks as project costs under the CA. CSS strongly objects to this recommendation, as EPA, through the direction of CSS' EPA Project Officer, expressly approved CSS' purchase of the pre-2007 MY trucks without retrofits as an eligible cost on the condition that they be retrofitted at a later date. At stated above, CSS is in the process of retrofitting the trucks and will be done with the retrofits by June 17, 2012.

> **OIG Response 20.** Our position on the recommendation remains unchanged. CSS did not provide during the audit or with its response to the draft report documentation showing EPA's approval of the purchase of the pre-2007 MY trucks. As discussed in **OIG Response 18**, we acknowledge that the EPA project officer confirmed with CSS that she was aware the process of retrofitting the trucks may take a "little bit of time." However, the retrofits for the pre-2007 MY trucks had not been completed even though almost 2 years had elapsed since the project officer confirmed her understanding of CSS' plan to upgrade the trucks with emission control equipment as of February 2012. With regard to CSS' comment that the truck retrofits will be completed by June 2012, the retrofits do not satisfactorily resolve the CA compliance issue with the pre-2007 MY trucks as discussed in **OIG Response 18**.

V. Comments on Chapter 5 – ARRA Job Reporting

The OIG Draft Report states that CSS' reporting of jobs created or retained with Recovery Act funds did not comply with OMB reporting guidance in two respects. First, CSS incorrectly included in its computations CSS labor hours funded with income from the revolving fund program. Second, it states that CSS reported as full-time equivalent (FTE) the positions of truck operators for trucks procured by CSS with Recovery Act funding and subsequently leased to the operators.

Since EPA's award of the CA to CSS in 2009, CSS has consistently sought guidance from EPA on how to comply with ARRA jobs reporting guidance. After EPA provided specific guidance on ARRA job calculation methodology to all ARRA grant recipients in October 2009, CSS proactively sought additional guidance from its EPA Project Officer on several specific questions unique to CSS about proper application of EPA's methodology. During those discussions, CSS and the EPA Program Office agreed upon a specific methodology that addressed

CSS' questions, pursuant to which CSS has reported its ARRA jobs created or retained figures. Although the ARRA jobs calculation methodology has been revised at least once, during the second quarter of the CA project period, EPA has approved each CSS quarterly report on Recovery Act jobs created or retained since 2009. Therefore, because CSS followed EPA's methodology and guidance, and because EPA was approving its ARRA jobs reports, CSS believed that the methodology it was using was appropriate and consistent with ARRA requirements.

Although CSS has been diligent in applying EPA's ARRA jobs calculation methodology, applying that methodology to the transactions incurred under the CA has always been challenging because the ARRA jobs methodology is inherently unclear. This is evidenced by OIG's own struggle to arrive at a conclusive interpretation of the ARRA methodology as applied to CSS' revolving loan fund during the OIG audit. During the audit, the OIG examiners initially believed CSS had understated its jobs figures, but later decided that CSS had overstated its jobs figures. Ultimately, the OIG examiners decided that almost none of the jobs CSS reported were eligible for Recovery Act purposes. CSS believes this interpretation of the ARRA jobs methodology is deficient, because it fails to capture the significant positive economic impacts that CSS' revolving loan fund has had, and continues to have, on thousands of independent truckers and small businesses. CSS believes it is beyond dispute that CSS' deployment of the CA funds has created or helped retain the jobs of scores of truckers throughout the United States. While CSS is willing to apply the ARRA jobs methodology as OIG and the Program Office decide, CSS strongly believes that the methodology should reflect as accurately as possible the actual, positive impacts that CSS has on the national economy.

> **OIG Response 21.** Our position remains unchanged. As discussed in the draft report, we were unable to confirm whether the EPA agreed with CSS' reporting methodology because the first project officer is no longer employed by the EPA. With regard to CSS' comment on EPA's approval of its ARRA reports, EPA staff did not verify that the number of jobs created or retained in the reports were correct and met the OMB guidance on Recovery Act quarterly reporting.
>
> We acknowledge that applying the OMB Recovery Act reporting guidance to CSS' revolving loan program expenditures under the CA has been challenging because the guidance provides only general instructions and criteria. However, the guidance does specify that recipients report the estimated number of jobs created or retained with Recovery Act funding. As discussed in the draft report, CSS included data for jobs that were not funded by the Recovery Act in its quarterly reports.

A. Labor Hours Funded with Income from the Revolving Loan Fund Program

The OIG Draft Report states that CSS incorrectly calculated the number of jobs created or retained for quarterly reports covering the period October 2009 through June 2010 because CSS included in those reports labor hours funded with income from the CSS' Revolving Loan Fund. The OIG Draft Report states that, under OMB reporting guidance, such labor hours should not have been included in the computation of the number of jobs created or retained because they were not funded under the Recovery Act.

CSS believes that were it not for the income generated by the loan fund, CSS would not have been able to maintain and/or add the staff it reported. Thus, even though CSS has not used CA funds directly for employee labor costs, it has used program income for such expenses. The CA calls for CSS to "use program income under the same terms and conditions of this agreement," so CSS believes that labor hours funded with CA program income should be reported in ARRA jobs calculations.[12] Conservatively, CSS believes the income derived from the CA funds in CSS' revolving loan fund has, over the course of the project period, created or preserved over 100 FTE positions for CSS staff. Thus, these labor hours are directly attributable to Recovery Act funds. As such, CSS reported these labor hours as jobs created with Recovery Act funds.

> **OIG Response 22.** We acknowledge CSS' comments on income generated by the revolving loan program. However, the OMB guidance on Recovery Act reporting specifies that recipients report the estimated number of jobs created or retained with Recovery Act funding as discussed in **OIG Response 21**. The CA programmatic condition cited in CSS' comments establishes the allowable and required usage of program income earned as a result of the EPA award. The programmatic condition does not pertain to the reporting of jobs created or retained with Recovery Act funds. As discussed in the draft report, CSS overstated the number of jobs created or retained in the quarterly reports in part because it included labor hours funded with program income.

B. FTE Truck Operator Positions

The OIG Draft Report also states that the full-time equivalent (FTE) positions of truck operators driving trucks procured by CSS with Recovery Act funding should not have been reported in CSS' ARRA job figures. The OIG Draft Report states that these positions should not have been included because the truck operators of the leased trucks are "beneficiaries" of Recovery Act funding, rather than "recipients" or "sub-recipients."

CSS disagrees with the OIG Draft Report's interpretation of the ARRA guidance. OMB requires that Recovery Act jobs be reported for sub-recipients, which OMB reporting guidance defines as "non-Federal entities that are awarded Recovery funding through a legal instrument from a Prime Recipient. Sub Recipients typically receive a contract, grant, or loan from the Prime Recipient to support performance of any portion of a project or program funded with Recovery dollars."[13] CSS believes that, because CSS only awards CA funds to its truck operators through legal instruments—namely, leases or conditional loans—these truck operators should constitute sub-recipients for purposes of ARRA reporting.

The OIG Draft Report, in excluding CSS customers from ARRA reporting figures, focused on the absence of the word "lease" from the OMB reporting guidance. CSS disagrees and notes that (a) leases are indisputably legal instruments; (b) the phrase "contract, grant, or loan" does not represent an exclusive list of legal instruments under which ARRA recipients can award funds to sub-recipients, and this is signaled by the presence of the word "typically"; and (c) interpreting the guidance to exclude these CSS customers is contrary to the intent of the

---

[12] CA, Programmatic Condition 12.
[13] OMB Guidance M-09-021, *Implementing Guidance for the Reports on Use of Funds Pursuant to the American Recovery and Reinvestment Act of 2009*.

Recovery Act, which requires CSS to, as accurately as possible, report the number of all jobs created or retained with Recovery Act funds.[14]

With the CA funds, CSS had, as of 12/31/2010, replaced or upgraded 1,148 trucks, and in so doing, created or preserved the jobs of at least as many drivers, loaders, maintenance, and dispatch staff. Using a conservative estimate of 1.5 jobs per truck, this means CSS created or preserved 1,722 jobs, at a cost of $5,226 in Recovery Act funding per job. Thus, thousands of truck drivers are in business and operating with clean and efficient diesel trucks because of the Recovery Act funds granted to CSS. Had CSS not provided a mechanism for these operators to stay in business, these jobs would have been lost and new jobs would not have been created.

OIG Response 23. We agree that leases are legal instruments. However, CSS did not provide Recovery Act funding to truck operators through lease agreements. According to CSS' records, it directly purchased trucks from wholesalers and fleets using Recovery Act funds. Therefore, wholesalers and fleets received Recovery Act funds. The truck operators benefitted from the Recovery Act funds through the truck lease agreements but did not receive Recovery Act funding. As discussed in the draft report, CSS overstated the number of jobs created or retained in the quarterly reports in part because it included FTE positions of operators for trucks procured with Recovery Act funds and subsequently leased to the operators.

C. CSS Response to OIG Recommendations

The OIG Draft Report recommends that EPA (a) assist CSS with developing an ARRA jobs reporting methodology that complies with OMB guidance; (b) correct past ARRA job reports with erroneous estimates; and (c) direct CSS to maintain corrected ARRA jobs documentation in its administrative records and submit any corrections to the federal government pursuant to future Recovery Act guidance.

While CSS disagrees with the OIG Draft Report's conclusions about CSS' job reporting figures, CSS stands ready to collaborate with the EPA Program Office to develop an ARRA job reporting methodology that is compliant with OMB guidance. Once the revised methodology is determined, CSS will recalculate and correct its prior ARRA quarterly reports, retain corrected jobs documentation in its administrative records, and submit updated reports to the federal government consistent with future Recovery Act guidance.

OIG Response 24. As discussed in the OIG responses above, our position remains unchanged on the jobs reporting issues discussed in the draft report. However, we agree that CSS should collaborate with EPA to develop a jobs created and retained reporting methodology that meets OMB Recovery Act guidance. CSS' planned actions to correct the reporting errors after the methodology is developed should satisfactorily address the recommendations.

---

[14] ARRA § 1512(c) requires that ARRA grant recipients report "an estimate of the number of jobs created and the number of jobs retained by the project or activity …."

Distribution

Assistant Administrator for Administration and Resources Management
Assistant Administrator for Air and Radiation
Director, Office of Grants and Debarment, Office of Administration and Resources Management
Director, Grants and Interagency Agreements Management Division, Office of Administration
    and Resources Management
Director, Office of Transportation and Air Quality, Office of Air and Radiation
Agency Follow-Up Official (the CFO)
Agency Follow-Up Coordinator
Associate Administrator for Congressional and Intergovernmental Relations
Associate Administrator for External Affairs and Environmental Education
Audit Follow-Up Coordinator, Office of Administration and Resources Management
Audit Follow-Up Coordinator, Office of Air and Radiation
Audit Follow-Up Coordinator, Office of Grants and Debarment, Office of Administration and
    Resources Management
Cascade Sierra Solutions, Chief Executive Officer